Ronald W. Stampfl
Elizabeth C. Hirschman

Theory in Retailing: Traditional and Nontraditional Sources

Proceedings Series

AMERICAN MARKETING ASSOCIATION

Dr. Ronald E. Goldsmith

Theory in Retailing: Traditional and Nontraditional Sources

Theory in Retailing: Traditional and Nontraditional Sources

Ronald W. Stampfl
University of Wisconsin-Madison

Elizabeth C. Hirschman
New York University

Proceedings Series AMERICAN MARKETING ASSOCIATION

222 South Riverside Plaza • Chicago, Illinois 60606 • (312) 648-0536

ⓒAmerican Marketing Association

1981

Printed in the United States of America

Cover Design by Mary Jo Krysinski

Library of Congress Cataloging in Publication Data

Theory in retailing.

    Includes bibliographies.
    1. Retail trade--Congresses. I. Stampfl, Ronald W.
II. Hirschman, Elizabeth.
HF5429.T42   658.8'7   80-23919
ISBN 0-87757-143-0

This Proceedings was published from camera-ready copy
prepared and submitted by the authors.

205/700/181

TABLE OF CONTENTS

List of Registrants   vii
Foreword   ix
Preface   xi

1. Criteria for Theory in Retailing - Robert Bartels   1

2. Perspectives on the Retailing of Services -
    Leonard L. Berry   9

3. Growth and Productivity Change in Retailing -
    Louis P. Bucklin   21

4. Managing the Retail Salesforce
    Gilbert A. Churchill, Jr., Neil M. Ford, and
    Orville C. Walker, Jr.   34

5. Portfolio Theory and the Retailing Life Cycle -
    William R. Davidson and Nancy E. Johnson   51

6. Retail Customer Satisfaction and Dissatisfaction -
    Stephen A. Greyser   64

7. Retailing and the Production of Popular Culture -
    Elizabeth C. Hirschman   71

8. Retailing Theory: Some Criticism and Some
    Admiration   - Stanley C. Hollander   84

9. A Review of Retail Store Experiments -
    Benjamin Lipstein   95

10. Retail Location Theory - David L. Huff   108

11. New Realities of Retail Management -
    Robert F. Lusch and Ronald W. Stampfl   122

12. Consumer Perceptions of Product Value -
    Joseph Barry Mason and Elizabeth Goldsmith   133

13. Product Positioning and Segmentation Strategy:
    Adaptable to Retail Stores? - Eleanor G. May   144

14. The Decision to Use Product Information at
    the Point of Purchase - J. Edward Russo   155

15. Retailing Theory: Perspectives and Approaches -
    Bert Rosenbloom and Leon G. Schiffman   168

16. A Theory of Merchandise Buying Behavior -
    Jagdish N. Sheth   180

LIST OF REGISTRANTS

Robert Bartels
Ohio State University

Leonard L. Berry
University of Virginia

Louis P. Bucklin
University of California

Gilbert A. Churchill, Jr.
University of Wisconsin

William R. Davidson
Management Horizons, Inc.

Richard C. Doran
SCOA Industries

Judith Ervin
Citicorp Retail Services

Neil M. Ford
University of Wisconsin

Stephen A. Greyser
Harvard University/MSI

Elizabeth C. Hirschman
New York University

Stanley C. Hollander
Michigan State University

David Huff
University of Texas

Nancy Johnson
Management Horizons, Inc.

Robert Kenmore
MKI Securities Corporation

William J. R. Lampe
Allied Stores Corporation

Fred Langrehr
Marquette University

Kent Larsson
General Mills

Paul Leblang
Saks Fifth Avenue

Walter K. Levy
Walter K. Levy Associates

Benjamin Lipstein
New York University

Robert Lusch
University of Oklahoma

Joseph B. Mason
University of Alabama

Eleanor G. May
University of Virginia

Bert McCammon
University of Oklahoma

James E. Mettee
City Products Corporation

Michael K. Mills
University of S. California

Gail A. Morrissey
SCOA Industries

Steven L. Osterweis
New York University

Allan L. Pennington
Dayton Hudson Corporation

David J. Rachman
Baruch College

Ruben Roca
Rouse Company

Bert Rosenbloom
Drexel University

Marvin J. Rothenberg
Retail Marketing Consultant

J. Edward Russo
University of Chicago

Leon G. Schiffman
Rutgers University

Jagdish N. Sheth
University of Illinois

Ravi Singh
Northwestern University

Ronald W. Stampfl
University of Wisconsin

Louis W. Stern
Northwestern University

Orville Walker
University of Minnesota

PREFACE

The papers comprising this volume were presented at a workshop held at New York University on April 24 and 25, 1980. Co-sponsored by the New York University Institute of Retail Management and the American Marketing Association, the meeting was attended by both academic researchers and their industry counterparts.

One of the major goals of the Institute of Retail Management is to foster communication between the academic community and retail executives—particularly those executives whose research must help top managements to set their companies' directions for the future. We believe the industry has much to gain from an exposure to the latest theoretical concepts and applications coming out of business faculties; similarly, we feel that the work of retailing theoreticians can only be strengthened by direct feedback from industry practitioners.

A complementary major goal of the American Marketing Association is to foster the development of theoretical and conceptual material in the several sub-areas of marketing.

As co-chairs of the workshop, it was our intent to support Institute and Association goals by inviting noted individuals of varied backgrounds to contribute theoretical or conceptual papers in the area of retailing. Some contributors had long-standing interest and backgrounds in retailing. Others, noted for their work in the varied sub-areas of marketing, were invited to turn their attention to retailing.

We are pleased that this approach provided a unique spectrum of contributors, and that the publication of this volume by the American Marketing Association will make the workshop papers available to a wide audience of retailers and scholars.

Ronald W. Stampfl
University of Wisconsin-Madison

Elizabeth C. Hirschman
New York University

CRITERIA FOR THEORY IN RETAILING

Robert Bartels, The Ohio State University

ABSTRACT

Insofar as any body of thought is based upon assumptions, it has a theoretical character. The peotentialities of theory development in retailing research, teaching, and practice have not been achieved because of overemphasis on its practicality. Conformity to the requirements of theory would alleviate this deficiency.

THE STANDARD OF "THEORY" AND "THEORIES"

A survey of titles of 175 books on retailing published from 1911 to 1974 revealed that not one included the word "theory." Eleven were designated as "principles." Otherwise, the subject was related to such terms as Management, Organization, Methods, Planning, Procedure, Problems, Fundamentals, Operations, Policy, and Techniques.

Does this imply that there is no theory in or of retailing, or that the retailing discipline is not theoretical? Not at all!

It does, however, raise some questions which should be considered prior to the subject of criteria for theory. First, is it possible to have theorization without the development of theory? It is, if by theorization is meant merely the process of reasoning, and if by theory is meant the development of a structured and cohesive body of thought as a result of that reasoning. There has been much "reasoning" concerning retailing, and a vast body of thought has been produced. That it has not been called "theory" suggests that its practical and descriptive nature has not consisted of "proof" of premises which constitute theory.

Second, is a "theory of retailing" distinct from "retailing theories"? By the latter are implied developed bodies or areas of thought concerning a number of retailing topics, such as store managment, location, pricing, etc. There are such theories. By "theory of retailing," on the other hand, is implied a comprehensive overview of retailing in general, of its macro character, of its place in general marketing, or of its role in our social structure. Such theorization has been fragmentary, and if the discipline has been deficient in any respect, it has been along this line.

Whether retailing thought develops along one line or another is a matter of scholars' choice. Marketing thought itself has been characterized by irrationalities resulting from ill-defined concepts, interdisciplinary borrowings, cultural myopia, and personal points of view. Retailing thought, too, has been shaped by scholars', preoccupation with

1

operational and managerial problems in the retailing laboratory. In both marketing and retailing, better balance in theory might have been achieved if the criteria for theory development had been appreciated. However, concern for metatheory, or the exposition of how theory is developed and evaluated, occurs only as a discipline matures. Its present surfacing in the study of retailing is wholesome evidence giving encouragement for better study, writing, and teaching of the subject.

Webster's International Dictionary defines "criteria" as "standards of judging; rules or tests, by which facts, principles, opinions, and conduct are tried in forming a correct judgment respecting them." In terms of this definition, five standards for retailing theory development are here proposed in a metatheory which has been useful in judging the broader theory of marketing in general. They are standards which pertain to the following:

1. Identification and definition of the subject
2. Integrity of thought structure
3. Diversity and variability of structural components
4. Dependent and independent relationships among variables
5. Generalization of relationships in a cohesive body of thought.

THE IMPORTANCE OF DEFINITION

As all theory is about a subject, the starting point in all theory development is precise conceptualization and definition of the subject. This is more than a rephrasing of an old concept or a redefinition with a novel twist. It should be a deep and searching attempt to indicate what the subject is "all about." With respect to retailing, if such a term has never been used, one might ask what is the activity that needs theorization or explanation. We have become too accustomed to thinking of it as selling to utimate consumers, as merchandising, as the creation of availability utility, as terminal assortment of consumer goods, as creation of a standard of living, or as management factors inherent in the operation of a retail store. Perhaps it should be recognized that retailing is a subset of marketing, and that one's concept of marketing inevitably conditions his concept of retail distribution (Figure 1).

In answer to the question "What is retailing?" one may speculate as to what is the role of this function in meeting of human consumption needs. To what extent is it a social as well as an economic process? Is it a macro as well as a micro process? Has it time and space dimensions? Is it independent of political ideologies, of degrees of economic development, of the state of the technological arts?

In theory development, subject definition serves as an hypothesis to be proved. If one says, "Retailing is ------," the remainder of his

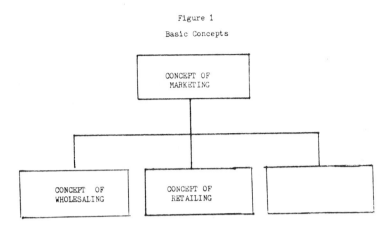

Figure 1

Basic Concepts

discourse should confirm this assertion. This would avoid proliferation of virtually identical texts and introduce meritorious distinctions with which one could agree or disagree. Every expository work is a theoretical piece; its assumptionns and definitions are implicit or explicit. If it attempts not to prove what retailing is -- or should be -- it falls not within the classification of theory, but is merely narrative or descriptive.

INTERNAL CONSISTENCY

As theory is a structure of thought, whatever the overall definition of the subject may be, everything in the thought structure should be implicit in that definition and should contribute to establishing the concept to be proved. This requires identification of subconcepts or categories in terms of which the subject is to be developed. For example, suppose that retailing were defined as the final stage of distribution logistics (Figure 2). The point to be proved may be that the logistics of supply processes is as applicable to civilian commodity distribution as to the support of military tactics. The categories of thought may then consist of coordinance of use and supply; functions of supply; alternative loci of the supply function; supply reserves relative to distance, time, and flow rates; and real versus opportunity costs under different plans of distribution. It is immediately apparent that theory cast in such a conceptual framework would be quite different from that based upon a definition of retailing as the shaping of consumption practices relative to the economic feasibility of the marketplace, or as a plausible position of command over the distribution channel.

Internal consistency is not a virtue of many retailing and marketing texts, especially in revised editions which are expanded, without redefinition, for the inclusion of new developments. Yet consistency

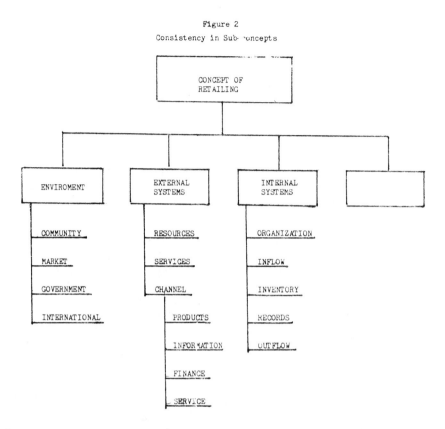

Figure 2

Consistency in Sub-Concepts

does not preclude inclusion of a number of topics, which in themselves may constitute a subject for theorization. Probably the broadest type of theory might be termed a Theory of Retailing,--a theory of what retailing in its entirety means. This is to be distinguished from Retailing Theories, or sub-topics which in themselves warrant theoretical exposition. Of such there may be many: Theories of Institutional Evolution, of Management in Environmental Change, of Pricing, of Store Layout, or of Merchandise Budgeting. All and more of such topics may be included in a comprehensive theory, provided that they all relate to and contribute to the overall plan for proving what retailing is really about.

Whatever the overriding concept of retailing may be, the implicit inherent categories of the subject must be consistent and coherent throughout.

UNIVERSALITY

Of the criteria for theory, the expectation of universality is one of the more elusive in marketing writings. Preoccupation is given to strategies for expanding, but not for contracting, markets; to large-scale retailing, but less to small-scale; to store atmosphere enrichment, but not to retrenchment; to advancing the Wheel of Retailing, but not to reversing it. Yet if theory or principles are worth acceptance they should apply equally to the entire range of possible circumstances. The theoretician must recognize this and employ metatheoretical logic to accommodate the quality of universality.

This is done by first differentiating between the types of categories previously identified, defined, and described, and the range or degrees of qualities which characterize any particular category. For example, department stores and grocery stores represent differences of kind in the institutional structure. But in both there are large stores and small stores, varying infinitely, representing differences of degree within the same kind. Depth of product line, advertising expenditures, customer loyalty, community expectations, sales commission, -- all exist at a point within a range of possible extremes.

This fact is taken into consideration in management as adjustment is made in response to changed circumstances or in expectation of change. This is done in expression of some principle or theory consciously or unconsciously held by the decision maker. It should be equally incorporated into the theorist's logic in order that all possible situations may be considered in formulating explanations of or prescriptions for retailing management. The same may be said of the theories of general marketing.

Graphically, these graduations within categories may represented as shown in Figure 3.

Figure 3

Intra-concept Range

PRODUCT LINE	CUSTOMER EXPECTATIONS	MARKET AREA	OPERATING COSTS
Deep	High	Local	High
----	----	----	----
----	----	----	----
----	----	----	----
----	----	----	----
----	----	----	----
----	----	----	----
----	----	----	----
----	----	----	----
----	----	----	----
Shallow	Low	Regional	Low

5

INFERENCE OF CAUSALITY

Arrayment of qualities is a step preliminary to the logical imputation of relationship among the categories, in which the variables are presumed to have dependence or independence relative to each other. This is the manner in which "causality" is inferred in the derivation of principles or laws of retailing behavior.

The presumption that there are marketing principles, of which retailing principles are a subset, supports the belief that there is retailing theory, although few retailing principles have been specifically identified, and confidence in the existence of retailing theory is low. A reason for this is that generalizations have been based largely upon relationships at one, rather than both, ends of the continuum of possible relationships, thus constituting rules of action, rather than universally valid principles. Interpreting what they read and are taught as simple prescriptions for success, students tend to disclaim that they know "theory" and have not the facility in management decision making which makes their understanding useful under widely different circumstances.

Graphically, the relationships may be represented as one factor being a function or derivative of another, and of their relationship being either direct or inverse. A widely accepted relationship has been popularly known as the Principle of Adaptivity, namely, that the composition and character of the retailing structure are a function or derivative of environmental circumstances. Another, that discount innovations in retailing are a function of market segments left unserved by the competitive tendency of service establishments to upgrade their offerings. Another, that store types and groupings are a function of shopping district distance from the city center. Some generalizations are oversimplified, and some that are offered as economic principles must be tempered in the light of social principles, as evidence from social and behavioral disciplines is incorporated into retailing thought.

Diagrammatically, the direct and inverse relationships in principles may be represented as in Figure 4.

SYNTHESIS OF THEORIES

The ultimate criterion for theory in retailing is whether theorization actually produces theories. Again, semantics is involved, for a theory to some people is an hypothesis; to others it is a cohesive body of principles concerning a given subject, and it is in this latter sense that it is here regarded. If a body of intelligence exists concerning either an area of retailing or retailing in its entirety, theory in retailing may be said to exist. (Figure 5).

6

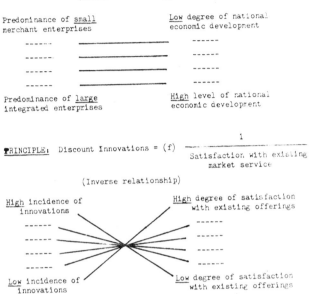

Figure 4

Relationships Among Concepts

PRINCIPLE: Retailing Structure = (f) Environmental Circumstances
(Direct relationship)

Predominance of small   Low degree of national
merchant enterprises   economic development

Predominance of large   High level of national
integrated enterprises   economic development

PRINCIPLE: Discount Innovations = (f) $\dfrac{1}{\text{Satisfaction with existing market service}}$

(Inverse relationship)

High incidence of   High degree of satisfaction
innovations   with existing offerings

Low incidence of   Low degree of satisfaction
innovations   with existing offerings

Considerable intelligence has been assembled throughout the development of marketing thought and the retailing literature to attest that our knowledge of retailing has both form and substance. That now questions should be raised concerning the existence of theory and the criteria for theory is evidence more of a reorganization of thought than an indication of starting anew along untrod paths. The need is for clear conception of what theory is and for precision in the conscious construction of theory. Many treatises on retailing are written largely from the standpoint of describing practice, of classifying factors, and of analyzing the elements of profit accounting. Case studies are often not carried to the point of generalization, but only to the solution of particular problems. Quantitative analysis may refine perceptions, but unless their subject is structured theoretically they may add little to the proof for which theory is designed.

7

Figure 5

Clusters of Principles in Theories

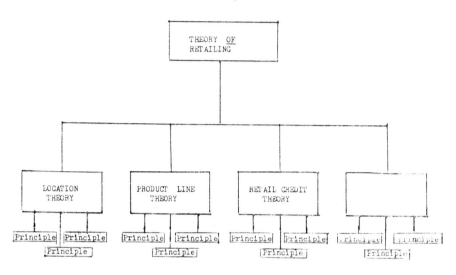

Theory in retailing is both desirable and possible. Conscious attention to it should benefit decision making by managers and public administrators. It should give perspective to the role of retailing in the community, in the distribution structure, and in society at large. It should assist in conveying retailing technology to nations looking to marketing as a means for economic development. And not the least, it should yield better writing, better teaching, and better comprehension on the part of students.

However the criteria for theory may be stated, standards are available for appraisal of our present achievements and for achievement of further goals. Our present concern for and consideration of them is an important step in the right direction.

PERSPECTIVES ON THE RETAILING OF SERVICES

Leonard L. Berry
McIntire School of Commerce
University of Virginia

ABSTRACT

Understanding the marketing characteristics and implications of services is important in retailing because almost all
retailers are involved with services to some degree. Key
service characteristics include intangibility, simultaneous
production and consumption, and the potential for variability.
Key marketing approaches include internal marketing, credibility building, tangibilizing the service, leveraging word-of-
mouth, and synchronizing supply and demand patterns.

INTRODUCTION

In some significant ways, the retailing of services is
different from the retailing of goods. The nature of these
differences, and the marketing implications they suggest, are
important for retailers to understand.

This paper examines some principal characteristics of
services, categorizes retailer involvement in services, and
suggests some of the marketing implications arising from these
considerations.[1]

CHARACTERISTICS OF SERVICES

Although service industries as a group are heterogeneous
(ranging from shoe shining to electric utilities), there are
certain characteristics of services about which it is useful
to generalize. Three of the most important of these characteristics are intangibility, simultaneous production and consumption, and the potential for service variability.

---

[1]Portions of this paper are drawn from Leonard. L. Berry
(1980), "Services Marketing Is Different," Business, (May-June),
pp. 24-29.

Intangibility

The most fundamental difference between a good and a service is that a good is an object and a service is a performance. When the consumer buys a good he or she acquires a tangible, something that can be seen, touched, perhaps worn or placed on a mantel. This is not the case when the consumer buys a service. Money has been spent but there are no additional clothes to hang in a closet and nothing to place on a mantel. As George writes: "After a day of buying services, the customer still has an empty market basket" (1977, p. 86).

Services are consumed but not possessed. Although the performance of most services is supported by tangibles, for example, the automobile in the case of a taxi service, the essence of what is being bought is a performance rendered by one party for another.

Intangibility has two meanings and both present challenges for marketing:

- that cannot be touched, impalpable.
- that cannot be easily defined, formulated, grasped, mentally (New World Dictionary, 1974, p. 731).

Simultaneous Production And Consumption

Services are generally produced and consumed in the same time frame. The college professor produces an educational service while the student consumes it. The telephone company produces telephone service while the telephone user consumes it. Generally, goods are produced, then sold, then consumed. Services on the other hand are usually sold first, then produced and consumed simultaneously.

Simultaneous production and consumption means that the service provider is often present when consumption takes place. Whereas an automobile might be manufactured in Michigan and consumed in Virginia, the dentist is present when examining a patient, the singer is present when performing a concert, the waiter is present when serving a restaurant meal.

What's important to recognize about the presence of the service provider is that the "how" of service distribution may greatly influence the customer's perception of the service. In the marketing discipline, great stress is placed on distributing goods to the "right place" and at the "right time." With services, it's often necessary to distribute them in the "right way" as well. How real estate agents, travel agents, physicians, lawyers, dance instructors, and bank tellers conduct themselves in the presence of the customer can influence future patronage decisions. Goods can't be rude or careless or thoughtless but people providing services can be and sometimes are. And when they are, the result may be a search for a new service supplier.

Potential For Variability

Service industries differ on the degree to which they are "people-based" or "equipment-based" (Thomas 1978). That is, there is a larger human component involved in performing some services (for example, jewelry appraisal) than other services (for example, telephone communications). One of the implications of this distinction is that the outcomes of people-based service operations tend to be less standardized and uniform than the outcomes of equipment-based service or goods-producing operations. Stated differently, the extensive involvement of people in the production of a service introduces a degree of variability in the outcome not present when machines dominate the production process. This is an important consideration since people-based service industries far out-number equipment-based service industries. Service variability occurs because service providers differ in their technical and customer-relation skills, personalities, and attitudes toward their work, and because the same service provider may provide differing levels of service quality from one service situation to the next.

The ever-present potential for variability in a labor-intensive service situation is well-known in the marketplace. Whereas consumers expect their favorite breakfast cereal to always taste the same, and to almost always hear a dial tone when picking up a telephone receiver, expectations are far less certain on the occasion of getting a haircut. This is why consumers look at their hair in a mirror prior to the hair-cutting service being concluded.

RETAILER INVOLVEMENT IN SERVICES

Understanding the characteristics of services is useful for retailers because virtually all of them offer services to one degree or another. As Levitt writes: "Everybody is in service" (1972, p. 42).

As noted in Figure I, retailers can be categorized as "goods retailers" or "service retailers" depending upon whether the thrust of the business is marketing objects (goods) or performances (services). This categorization is acceptable only insofar as it is recognized that most goods retailers offer services.

FIGURE I

TYPES OF RETAILER INVOLVEMENT IN SERVICES

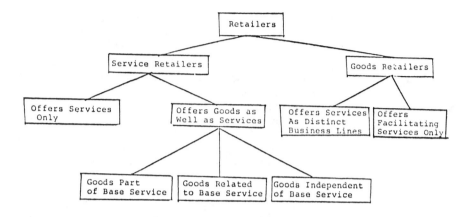

Goods Retailers

Some goods retailers offer services as distinct business lines; others restrict service offerings to those that facilitate the sale of goods. Concerning the former, it has been estimated that as much as 20 percent of department store revenues will come from services by 1990.[2] Encouraging the increasing involvement of goods retailers with services as distinct business lines are the growth forecasts for the services sector of the economy, the desire to further capitalize on existing organizational talents and strengths, the marketing potential of more fully serving customer needs, and the prospects that services will increase store traffic, sales of related merchandise, and institutional distinctiveness.

Woll (1975) provides an illustrative list of services offered for sale by goods retailers: insurance, photo studios, beauty salons, appraisal, monogramming, interior decorating, shop-at-home services, rug cleaning, appliance and furniture repair at home, ticket brokerage and tool rentals.

In addition to offering services as distinct business lines, goods retailers also offer services to facilitate the sale of goods. Common "facilitating" services include bagging,

---

[2] As cited in Bernard Wysocki, Jr, (1978), "Major Retailers Offer Varied Services to Lure Customers, Lift Profits," Wall Street Journal (June 12), p. 1.

check cashing, credit, wrapping, delivery, information, and product repair and maintenance.

Service Retailers

As shown in Figure I, service retailers also fall into two broad groupings: those that offer services only and those that offer goods as well as services. Service retailers offering goods are further categorized according to whether the goods are part of the base service, related to the base service, or independent of the base service.

Examples of service retailers offering goods as part of the base service include rental outlets and restaurants, i.e., goods are rented and eaten. Examples of service retailers offering goods related to the base service include travel agencies selling travel gear and beauty salons selling haircare products. Examples of service retailers offering goods independent of the base service include airlines selling a variety of unrelated items through catalogues and film developing outlets renting video cassette entertainment programs. It is possible of course for a service retailer to offer goods fitting more than one of these sub-classifications.

Examples of service retailers offering services only are numerous and include intra-city transportation providers (taxi, bus, subway), companies offering speed-reading courses, appraisers, concert promoters, and dry cleaners.

HIGH AND LOW CONTACT RETAILERS

It is useful to classify retailers not only according to whether they primarily offer goods or services but also according to the extent of contact they have with customers. Figure II classifies retailers into four sub-groups: High contact service retailers, high contact goods retailers, low contact service retailers, and low contact goods retailers.[3] High contact retailers are characterized by considerable interaction between retailer personnel and customers. Low contact retailers are characterized by minimal interaction between personnel and customers.

Examples of high contact service retailers include banks, airlines, and real estate agencies. Examples of high contact

---

[3]The terminology "high contact" and "low contact" is drawn from Richard B. Chase (1978), "Where Does The Customer Fit In A Service Operation," Harvard Business Review, (November-December), pp. 137-142.

FIGURE II

HIGH AND LOW CONTACT RETAILERS

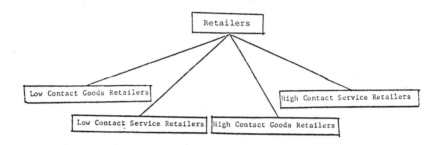

goods retailers include conventional department stores, certain types of specialty stores, and door-to-door retailers. Examples of low contact service retailers include electric utilities, dry cleaners and movie theaters. Examples of low contact goods retailers include supermarkets, catalogue retailers, and vending machine operators.

High contact goods and service retailers are purposely linked together in Figure II because both types of retailers are heavily reliant on personnel quality and performance to realize marketing objectives. Accordingly, in some ways high contact service retailers confront problems more like those of high-contact goods retailers than low-contact service retailers.

MARKETING IMPLICATIONS

The relative importance of various marketing concepts and tools, and how they are used, may differ depending upon whether a good or service is being marketed and whether there is high or low contact with customers. This section suggests some of these differences.

Internal Marketing

For low contact service retailers, equipment tends to predominate and personnel tend to come into contact with customers during the less crucial segments of the consumption act, e.g., taking tickets at a movie theater. The same is basically true for low contact goods retailers because of their self-service character.

For high contact service retailers, the quality of the service is inseparable from the quality of the service provider. A rude waiter can ruin what otherwise might have been perceived as a "fine meal." A testy stewardess means to the consumer a testy airline. The quality of personnel performance is also important to high contact goods retailers because considerable contact often occurs during crucial stages of the buying process when personnel competence, friendliness and enthusiasm can make a sale and help solidify customer loyalty to the store and when the absence of these attributes can have the opposite effect.

A key difference between high contact goods and service retailers is that the goods retailer may be able to survive mediocre or even poor personnel performance if its merchandise is sufficiently in demand. Such is not likely to be the case with service retailers who, in many cases, market nothing other than personnel performance.

Although low contact retailers certainly cannot afford to ignore personnel issues, these matters are not nearly the marketing priority for them that they are for high-contact retailers. To become better marketers, it is especially important that high-contact retailers be concerned with internal marketing[4] not just external marketing.

Internal marketing means applying the philosophy and practices of marketing to the people-resources that serve the external customer so that (1) the best possible people can be employed and retained, and (2) they will do the best possible work. More specifically, internal marketing is viewing employees as internal customers, viewing jobs as internal products, and, just as with external marketing, endeavoring to design these "products" to better meet the needs of these "customers" (Thompson, Berry, and Davidson, 1978, p. 243).

Although most executives are not accustomed to thinking of marketing in this way, the fact is that people do "buy" jobs from employers and employers can and do use marketing to "sell" these jobs on an initial and ongoing basis. To the extent that high-contact retailers use the concepts and tools of marketing to offer better, more satisfying jobs, they upgrade their capability for being more effective retailers.

The relevance of marketing thinking to personnel management is very real. Marketing research can be used to identify employee needs and attitudes just as it can be used to uncover consumer needs and attitudes. Employee markets can and should

---

[4]Technically the phrase "internal marketing" can be applied to any form of marketing inside an organization. In this paper, the phrase concerns marketing to employees.

be segmented and indeed it is the accommodation of individual differences that is behind the growing popularity of such personnel actions as "flexitime" and "cafeteria benefits." Advertising and other communications programs can be designed to educate and motivate those internal to the firm as well as those external.

Using Price As A Clue

Because goods are tangible and can be seen and touched they are generally easier for a consumer to evaluate than services. The intangibility of services encourages consumer attention to "clues" associated with a service for help in assessing its nature and quality.

The tendency for customer-prospects to use the price of a good as an indicator of its quality is well-known. Eiglier and Langeard (1977) suggest, however, that this tendency is even more pronounced for services. They argue that the relative absence of material data with which to appraise services makes price a potentially important index of quality.

Consumers can be expected to use price as a clue in circumstances where they anticipate differences in service quality from one supplier to another and where the personal risk of buying a lower quality service is high. It follows that lawyers, accountants, investment counselors, consultants, convention speakers and hair stylists can contradict signals they wish to communicate about quality by setting their prices too low. In short, price can be a confidence builder.

Capitalizing On Existing Credibility

Just as price can add credibility concerning a service's quality, so can distributing the service through a goods-retailing organization that already has credibility. That is, the consumer who has confidence in a particular retailer because of past experiences with the firm and its products may be willing to transfer these expectations to services the retailer adds. There is little doubt, for instance, that the automotive service and insurance business lines at Sears have benefited greatly from the association with the Sears' name and reputation for quality merchandise.

In a recent paper, George (1977, pp. 88-89) portrays the potential benefits of tying services marketing into a goods-marketing organization with a hypothetical scenario involving an established department store adding a health spa:

> The store's strengths include a loyal market
> of middle age, upper middle class, upper
> income customers . . . a reputation for

quality; and an image of progressive merchandising . . . . The health spa industry, in
general, has a poor image which includes
high pressure telling tactics, poor quality
personnel, and inattention once the sale has
been made. The new offering's intangibility
allows the store to use its positive image to
reduce the uncertainty and perceived risks for
potential users of the spa. In addition to
revenues generated from the spa services, there
are many possibilities for cross-selling other
stores lines such as sporting goods, sportswear,
and health food products.

Interestingly, the process can work the other way with
well-known and well-regarded service companies moving into
goods marketing. The key is where the credibility and access
to the customer lies. In the above scenario it lies with the
department store. In the case of service enterprises like
American Express and TWA it lies with them.

Tangibilizing The Service
Tangibility provides goods with a number of marketing
advantages over services. Goods can be displayed on a shelf
or rack, contained in packages that serve as "silent salesmen,"
pictured in advertising, sold and distributed through the mail,
and effectively branded. These are not insignificant matters
and help account for the vastly different visual experience
the consumer has when visiting Bloomingdales instead of Citi-
bank or when reading a Saks Fifth Avenue advertisement instead
of an American Airlines advertisement.

Because of the marketing advantages of tangibility,
retailers should consider whether there are opportunities to
tangibilize the services they offer.[5]

Sometimes it is possible to make a service more palpable
by creating a tangible representation of it. This is what has
occurred with the development of the bank credit card. By
tangibly representing the service with a plastic card, Visa
and others have been able to overcome many of the handicaps
normally associated with marketing an intangible. The
existence of the plastic card has allowed Visa to physically
differentiate the service through color and graphics and to

---

[5]This section is based on James H. Donnelly, Jr. (1980)
"Service Delivery Strategies in the 1980's - Academic Perspec-
tive," in Leonard L. Berry and James H. Donnelly, Jr. (eds.),
Financial Institution Marketing: Strategies in the 1980s,
Washington, D.C.: Consumer Bankers Association, pp. 143-150.

build and even extend a potent brand name, e.g., Visa travelers checks. Moreover, banks distributing Visa cards can extend their trading areas because once the card is obtained by consumers (which can be handled through the mail) credit purchases can be made without going to the bank.

Just as retailers should consider whether there are opportunities to develop a tangible representation of the service, so should they consider whether there are opportunities to make the service more easily grasped mentally. For example, the insurance industry has made it easier for consumers to mentally grasp what is being sold by associating the intangible of insurance with relevant tangible objects. Consider the following:

- "You are in good <u>hands</u> with Allstate."
- "I've got a piece of the <u>rock.</u>"
- "Under the Traveler's <u>umbrella.</u>"
- "The Nationwide <u>blanket</u> of protection."

Hands, rocks, umbrellas and blankets are used to more effectively communicate what insurance can provide people; they are devices used to make the service more easily grasped mentally.

Leveraging Word-of-Mouth

The ever-present potential for variability in the provision of labor-intensive services contributes to the important role word-of-mouth communications plays in consumer selection of service suppliers. To find the right doctor, automobile mechanic, hairdresser, attorney, college teacher, real estate agent, or travel bureau, the consumer asks others who have already tested the water, others without vested interest in the selection made. As Eiglier and Langeard (1977, p. 43) write: "The phenomenon of word-of-mouth, as well as the influence of opinion leaders, probably assumes a considerable importance for services; these two elements are . . . one of the means of reducing the difficulties that the consumer encounters: His problem of confidence, his problem of the first test . . . ." The research of Davis, Guiltinan and Jones (1979), Green, Langeard, and Favell (1974), and Seaton and Vogel (1977) all suggest the importance of word-of-mouth communications in selecting service suppliers.

The propensity for word-of-mouth communications in service markets suggests that a key marketing strategy might be to attempt to leverage this propensity. Making a conscious effort to encourage word-of-mouth might simply mean writing thank you letters to the sources of favorable communications when identified. It might mean aggressive marketing to opinion leaders. It might mean developing communications materials that customers and employees could make available to non-customers. How to operationally encourage word-of-mouth communications in service markets is a useful research issue for the 1980's.

Synchronizing Supply And Demand

Because services are performances capacity management tends to be a particular challenge in the retailing of services. If an airline has 40 more flight reservation requests than capacity permits, some business will likely be lost. Conversely, if an airliner takes off with 40 empty seats, the revenue that those seats could have produced, had they been filled, is lost foreover.

Confronting many retailers of services is the need to find ways to better synchronize supply and demand as an alternative to recurring conditions of severe overdemand and underdemand. This is easier said than done. Demand peaks can occur during certain times of the day (airlines, restaurants), certain days of the week (movies, hair styling), and certain months of the year (income tax services, beach resorts) (Sasser, 1976).

To better synchronize supply and demand the retailer may attempt to change demand patterns for the service, supply patterns, or both (Sasser, 1976). It may be possible to alter demand patterns through changes in product strategy (fast-food chains adding breakfast), distribution strategy (banks adding automatic teller machines), promotion strategy (professional sports teams using special promotions for middle-of-the-week games) and pricing strategy (car rental companies offering reduced weekend rates).

Supply capacities may be altered by substituting equipment for labor to make the service system more productive (automated car wash) and by various personnel actions (cross-training employees to perform multiple jobs and employing part-time and para-professional personnel).

CONCLUSION

Understanding the marketing characteristics and implications of services is useful for retailers because virtually all retailers are involved with services to some extent. Among the key characteristics of services are intangibility, simultaneous production and consumption, and the potential for variability. These characteristics suggest the significance of such marketing approaches as internal marketing, credibility

19

building, tangibilizing the service, encouraging word-of-mouth communications, and synchronizing supply and demand patterns.

Service retailing is different from goods retailing in some important ways. Those goods retailers extending their involvement in services in the eighties will be well advised to make the effort to fully understand these differences.

REFERENCES

Davis, Duane L., Joseph P. Guiltinan, and Wesley H. Jones (1979), "Service Characteristics, Consumer Search, and the Classification of Retail Services," Journal of Retailing, 55 (Fall), 3-23.

Eiglier, Pierre and Eric Langeard (1977), "A New Approach to Service Marketing," in Eiglier, et al., Marketing Consumer Services: New Insights, Cambridge: Marketing Science Institute.

George, William R. (1977), "The Retailing of Services - A Challenging Future," 53 Journal of Retailing (Fall), 85-98.

Green, R.T., Eric Langeard, and A.C. Favell (1974), "Innovation in the Service Sector: Some Empirical Findings," Journal of Marketing Research, 11 (August), 323-326.

Levitt, Theodore (1972), "Production - Line Approach to Service", Harvard Business Review, 50 (September-October), 41-52.

New World Dictionary of the American Language (1974), Second Edition, 731.

Sasser, W. Earl (1976), "Match Supply And Demand in Service Industries," Harvard Business Review, 54 (November-December), 133-140.

Seaton, Bruce and Ronald H. Vogel (1977), "A Replication Study of Innovation in the Service Sector," in Contemporary Marketing Thought, Proceedings of the Fall Educators Conference of the American Marketing Association, 370-374.

Thomas, Dan R.E. (1978), "Strategy is Different in Service Businesses," Harvard Business Review, 56 (July-August), 158-165.

Thompson, Thomas W., Leonard L. Berry, and Philip H. Davidson (1978), Banking Tomorrow - Managing Markets Through Planning, New York: Van Nostrand Reinhold.

Woll, Milton (1975), "Merchandising Services - Planning for the Next Decade," Stores (May), 6-7, 35-36.

GROWTH AND PRODUCTIVITY CHANGE IN RETAILING

Louis P. Bucklin, University of California, Berkeley

ABSTRACT

This article shows growth in consumer demand to play a dominant role in the stimulation of higher retail productivity and, most probably, the dissemination of new retail technology. Therefore, unless consumer demand resumes its former growth, or new means are derived to diffuse the technology, productivity growth in retailing may continue its recent meager performance.

INTRODUCTION

Research over the past thirty years has shown the field of retailing to consistently lag manufacturing in the growth of labor productivity (Barger 1955; Cox 1965; Bucklin 1978). Recent statistics published through the Bureau of Labor Statistics continue to indicate this pattern. For the field of retailing, between 1958 and 1977, the rate of growth was approximately 1.55 percent per annum. For the manufacturing industries studied by the Bureau, the rate was 2.80 for a difference of something better than 1 percent (Monthly Labor Review 1979). This gap has commonly appeared in previous studies.

For the period of 1973 to 1977, however, retail productivity grew at the negligible amount of .10 per annum compared to 1.52 for manufacturing industries (Monthly Labor Review 1979). Various indicators for 1978 show further weakness in retailing productivity in several sectors, suggesting that average growth in efficiency over the previous five-year period was probably negative. While manufacturing is also suffering from the general decline in output in the economy, retailing has been especially impacted.

These developments raise the issue of whether retailing is more dependent than manufacturing upon growth as a means of technology diffusion and, if so, what implications this may have for continuing productivity development in trade. The question is especially critical because of the possibility for persistent low growth in constant dollar retail sales. This low growth emanates not only from a diminished birth rate and negligible gains in real income, but from a continuing shift in personal expenditures from products to services. With housing expense rising more rapidly than many other living costs, the shift of income to the purchase of services may become more severe.

Research in the process of technological change has, of course, long shown a relationship between output growth and productivity in an industry. Kendrick studied this relationship in manufacturing for the period 1948 to 1969 (1973). Across twenty-one manufacturing groups, he found the following relationship, where P and O are annual rates of change for productivity and the t-score underneath the coefficient in parentheses.

$$P = 2.113 + .285 \ 0, \qquad R^2 = .29. \qquad (1)$$
$$(3.3)$$

Equation (1) indicates that 28.5 percent of output growth is translated into productivity growth. Since output growth traditionally has exceeded that of productivity, a large proportion of gains in productivity may therefore be traced to changes in demand. While the degree of explanation is not strong in equation (1), R squared equals .29, this is largely due to missing variables (which when present strengthen both R and the t-score (Kendrick 1973).

In retailing, Schwartzman's work shows that the same forces are at work (1971). For the ten retail groups he examined during 1929 to 1963, a regression comparable to that of Kendrick's reveals that

$$P = .294 + .388 \ 0, \qquad R^2 = .41. \qquad (2)$$
$$(2.4)$$

This indicates that the association between retail output and labor productivity is both stronger than in manufacturing, i.e., the coefficient is .10 points higher, and that growth explains a greater proportion of the variance in productivity. The sample size of ten, however, leaves much to be desired with respect to the confidence with which this statement can be made.

The current availability of productivity data for several retail trades over time now makes it possible to undertake further research on this issue. First, the extent to which growth of output does serve as a, or possibly, "the" major force in the growth of productivity may be determined. The second is whether this relationship varies across different retail trade types. Data are derived from the Bureau of Labor Statistics' recently initiated annual studies of productivity growth in selected retail trades (Bureau of Labor Statistics 1979). To the date of this essay, reports were available upon four retail types: food stores, new car dealers, service stations, and eating and drinking places. Productivity data derived by me from National Retail Merchants Association publications permit the addition of department stores to this group (Controller's Congress 1963-1978).

In order to fully specify the nature of the relationship between output and productivity growth, information for a greater number of retail types as well as related data on factors associated with productivity change is necessary. While this study undertakes some of this, the incompleteness and roughness of data for these other factors require that the report be labeled exploratory.

CONCEPTUAL FRAMEWORK

Theoretically, one should expect a strong, causal relationship between output and productivity growth and for this to vary across different retail types.

Output Growth and Productivity

With strong demand, additional capacity is required to supply the product or the service. The new capacity permits the installation of the latest technology and the consequent advancement of productivity. The faster the rate of growth, the greater the opportunity for new technologies to diffuse. In addition, output growth should have a buoyant impact upon industry profits and provide ample capital for the replacement of existing facilities. For industries with declining demand, the converse will be true. Here the problem is to rid the industry of capacity currently in place. Sunk costs, however, often delay the removal of even obsolete facilities.

Growth of output has both shorter and longer term effects. In the very short run, greater demand allows more intensive resource use. This is especially true in retailing where additional volume can often be accommodated with only marginal stress through use of queues in the provision of service. Conversely, with declining demand it is often difficult to reduce resource commitments rapidly.

In the longer term, heavy demand ought to produce strong incentive for supplier industries to innovate. In effect, the profit-motivating forces at the user industry level are passed back to the supply channel, stimulating technology and providing further incentive for productivity gain. Conversely, in declining industries interest in providing new technologies, especially of a specialized nature, may all but disappear.

Moving to a different perspective, it may be argued that causation in the relationship also runs in the opposite direction. Industries with faster productivity growth will usually

23

provide either relatively better prices or improved services over time. Hence, buyers are more likely to expand their purchases of these products thereby extending the growth in their demand. In this manner, technological growth may provide the basis for its continuance through the generation of higher demand growth rates and, thereby, facilitate its diffusion. The detection of these reciprocal effects is not a simple task and will not be undertaken in this paper.

The Effect of Output Growth Across Different Retail Types

Whether output growth in demand will have the same effect for all industries is a facet of productivity change that has not been raised in the literature. However, from a conceptual point of view, not only does this effect seem possible, but highly likely. Two conditions account for this. The first is the extent to which construction of totally new facilities is required for technological advance. The second relates to the ease of exit of obsolete capacity.

In some industries modification of the existing plant may be sufficient to enable new equipment to be installed. In others, new facilities of different size or configuration are required. The latter is especially likely to be true where establishments are expanding to take advantage of scale or product line economies, such as supermarkets. Or as in grocery warehouses, the older facilities were built with ceilings too low to accommodate modern materials handling equipment.

All of this might make little difference if space for the construction of new facilities were readily available. However, because some industries are more market oriented than others, the ease of finding open space may vary. Supermarkets, for example, were able to find the space through the abandonment of city facilities for new suburban stores. On the other hand, prior to the evolution of suburban shopping centers, department stores were constrained in their expansion to the central business districts in which they were located. These districts have migrated over time, permitting some new stores to be built, but this is a glacial process. Demolition and rebuilding has been an extraordinarily costly and usually prohibitive option. Growth has more often required that adjacent buildings be acquired and patched together to form the enlarged establishment. The stronger market dependence of the department store has meant, therefore, that optimal replacement of facilities has not been possible. Hence, productivity growth will suffer.

Indeed, in general, central city retailing has often retained its historic structure over long periods of time. It is commonplace to note that retailing in older sections of cities is conducted in stores of different types and size than in newer developments. Because retail types vary in their degree of market dependence, e.g., shopping versus convenience stores, those most vulnerable will require the formation of new population centers in order to introduce the newest technology. Parenthetically, market dependence may also be the major factor that distinguishes between the retailing and manufacturing in their dependence upon demand growth for the introduction of technological change.

The ease by which industry facilities can exit is the second condition affecting productivity growth. When an obsolete plant can be converted to other uses, then abandonment costs are low and change is facilitated. Conversely, where unique building features cause renovation for other purposes to be expensive, then obsolete and obsolescent facilities will be retained over a longer period of time. Productivity in industries of this type should, therefore, grow at a lower rate.

Department stores, for example, are a retail trade where exit is difficult. The scale of historic downtown facilities is such that other retail uses are difficult to find. Conversion to office facilities is possible, but ill suited and expensive. Hence, capacity has little alternative use and is retained as long as revenues exceed current costs. On the other hand, small specialty stores can often move in and out of a variety of facilities. Bicycle or ski shops utilize relatively simple shops that are common across a number of uses, both retailing, service, and office. The introduction of new facilities, or the exit of old, is greatly simplified and productivity growth should be possible without growth in output.

Other Factors Affecting Productivity Growth

Before leaving the conceptual area, a few comments are appropriate with respect to other factors that might affect productivity growth in retailing. Unless these are specified in a statistical model of productivity growth, then interpretations of the role of expansion in demand may be in error if these other factors are correlated with changes in output.

For example, expansion in establishment size may accompany growth in output. If economies of scale are being realized in this process, then the number of establishments in a given trade may be inversely associated with productivity growth. If this variable is important, and associated with output growth, then any coefficient reflecting the latter will be reduced if establishment size is omitted from the model.

The number of other potential factors affecting productivity change is large and correlation with output unknown. Hence, unbiased estimates of the effect of output growth cannot be derived without much data development and testing. Some possible contributors are the extent of unionization, the quality of labor employed, and the degree to which consumer services can be abandoned.

Certain retail types, for example, may be more susceptible to union activities, e.g., establishments such as supermarkets, department stores, and automotive dealers. Union activities, where effective in raising wages, may lead management to introduce more labor-saving devices. Cross-sectional studies have shown, for example, that higher wage rates are associated with higher labor productivity levels (Bucklin 1978, p. 76).

Union activity may, however, effectively counter these efforts by tactics that delay the introduction of new equipment. Union opposition to the use of scanning equipment in food stores and, probably, to pre-cut meats has slowed exploitation of these new technologies and productivity gains. Such constraints may be higher in declining industries than in those expanding. An interaction variable may be required to detect this phenomenon.

In some trades, the abandonment of service poses an especially severe problem to the productivity analyst. Service reduction also diffuses through time and often requires the introduction of new technologies--witness the development of expensive information processing centers for self-service checkout in supermarkets and gasoline stations. Output growth will consequently be associated with increases in efficiency as well as reductions in service levels and its role in each may be difficult to disentangle. Without accurate measure of service levels at retail, a task which remains to be achieved, the specific effect of output change upon real productivity growth may be overstated. Qualitative evaluation of developments in different retail trades provides the only current basis for analysis.

Given this perspective, the specific questions of interest may be presented more formally. These are:

1) Output growth in retailing accounts for a significant and high proportion of productivity growth.

2) Output growth has a dissimilar effect upon productivity growth in different retail types.

3) The role of output growth will be less where economies of scale and/or wages are rising rapidly.

EMPIRICAL ESTIMATION

To determine the effect of output change upon productivity, annual productivity data for five retail trade types from 1958 to 1976 were transformed to first difference index numbers and pooled. This transformation reduced the intense serial correlation found in statistical models for annual data and standardized values across different data sets. Pooling provides the basis for considering whether relationships among variables are similar across the different retail types. The statistical model employed to evaluate the data was ordinary least squares.

The Role of Growth

The results of the regression of output growth upon productivity change for the pooled data are shown in equation (3) where apostrophes indicate first differences and t-scores are in parentheses.

$$P' = 52.34 + .4860\ 0', \qquad \text{Adj } R^2 = .37, n = 90. \qquad (3)$$
$$(7.6) \qquad (7.3)$$

This shows that approximately one-half of every percentage point of output change is translated into productivity growth in the five retail trades, considerably higher than the cross-sectional coefficients found by both Kendrick and Schwartzman. Because the average output growth of the five retail trades during the period was 3.5 percent per annum, this means that 1.7 points of the average productivity change index of 102.64 may be attributed to output growth $(102.64 - (52.34 + 100 \times .4860))$. If demand had remained constant, e.g., for $0'$ to be 100, the regression forecasts a mean productivity change index of .94 percent per annum. Interestingly, low as this is, it still exceeds recent retail growth rates.

Differences Among the Retail Trades

Table 1 shows the differences in productivity growth rates for the five retail trades. The table ranks the five by the average annual percentage increase in demand over the period from 1959 to 1976. For each trade but one, change in output was greater than change in productivity. There was also a rough relationship between output and productivity growth; however, the restaurant trade did not conform to this pattern.

Whether the relationships in the pooled data are homogeneous across the five retail types may be determined by adding dummy variables in the regression model to represent constant and variable coefficients for each of the retail trade types. This "complete difference" model is equivalent to running equation (3) separately for each of the five retail types. The appropriate method for determining whether the coefficients are

27

similar is an F-test of the residual sum of squares for equation (3) on the pooled data versus the sum of the residual sum of squares derived from running equation (3) separately for each retail type (Rao and Miller 1971).

TABLE 1

RELATIVE PRODUCTIVITY PERFORMANCE OF FIVE
RETAILER TYPES, 1959-1976

Retail Type	Output		Productivity	
	Rank	Rate	Rank	Rate
New car dealers	1	3.40[a]	2	2.15[a]
Service stations	2	3.03	1	3.43
Restaurants	3	2.86	5	0.74
Department stores	4	2.20	4	1.61
Food stores	5	2.15	3	1.71

[a]Annual rate of growth in percent.

With an $F(8,80)$ of 2.97 this test indicated that there was a better than 99 percent chance that some, or all, of the coefficients were different among the five retail types. Evaluation of which coefficient(s) was the source of the variance was undertaken by running the statistical model with dummy variables for individual alpha and beta coefficients for each of the different trades.

This search for an improved model was aided greatly by table 1 which indicates that the trades that departed the most from the overall pattern were service stations and restaurants. Although all possible combinations of dummy variables were not reviewed, equation (4) as shown below with mnemonic subscripts for the dummies, explained a substantially higher proportion of the variance. The $F(5,80)$ ratio between this regression, and the complete difference model, was .58. Since this ratio is not significant at any reasonable level of probability, the three new variables exhaust the bulk of the unexplained variance between equation (3) and the complete difference model.

$$P' = 48.05 + 27.09_{ss} - 1.636_{rs} + .5275\ 0' - .2453\ 0'_{ss} \quad (4)$$
$$(6.9) \quad (1.7) \quad (2.6) \quad (7.8) \quad (1.6)$$
$$\text{Adj } R^2 = .48, \quad n = 90$$

The new variables were dummy constants for service stations and restaurants and a dummy output growth variable for the former. For service stations the relationship between output

28

growth was diminished by approximately 50 percent, as derived
by adding the dummy output coefficient, $0'_{ss}$ to $0'$. Again
assuming a no-growth situation, and substituting 100 for the
$0'$ variables in equation (4), one projects a productivity
growth for service stations of 3.4 percent per annum.

The addition of these variables also altered the effect of
output growth for the other three retail types. Comparing $0'$
between equations (3) and (4) shows it to have increased by
almost 4 percentage points. With the exception of restaurants,
productivity growth would be at the .8 level for the remainder
of the retail trades (derived by adding the constant to the no-
growth representation of $0' \times 100$). Restaurants, however, lose
efficiency at about .8 percent per year unless there are regular increases in output (P'_{rs} = .992).

Economies of Scale
The exploitation of economies of scale in retailing, as
discussed above, may be correlated with output growth and affect the coefficient. This potential was evaluated through the
addition of a variable on the number of establishments in each
of the several trades, except department stores. Department
stores were omitted from the pooled data as information for establishments was not available from the NRMA source.

With number of establishments included in the regression
equation, and output levels held constant, this new measure reflects the operating size of the average establishment. A significant negative coefficient indicates the existence of economies of scale.

Equation (5) is based upon the data pooled across the four
retail types for productivity, output, and establishment size.

$$P' = 97.66 + .5478 \ 0' - .5212 \ E', \quad \text{Adj } R^2 = .43, \ n = 72 \quad (5)$$
$$\quad (6.5) \quad \ (8.4) \quad \quad (3.5)$$

The addition of establishments proved to be significant, improving the explanatory power of the model over that of equation (3). The high b coefficient of .52 for the number of establishments in equation (5) indicates that for every 1 percent
annual reduction, an increase of almost .5 percent in trade
productivity may be achieved.

The test between equation (5) and the complete difference
model, $F(9,60)$ with the two independent variables, is highly
significant. Prime candidates are dummy variables for the restaurant and service stations. With some experimentation, the
following equation was derived. It includes dummy constants
for restaurants and service stations and a dummy variable

coefficient for the number of service station establishments.

$$P' = 42.75 \overset{.}{+} 111.44_{ss} - 1.67_{rs} + .5792\ 0' - 1.1033\ E'_{ss} \quad (6)$$
$$(7.7) \quad (5.6) \quad (3.1) \quad (10.7) \quad (5.5)$$
$$\text{Adj } R^2 = .68, \quad n = 72$$

The $F(7,60)$ of .48 between equation (6) and complete difference model indicates that this also exhausts most of the unexplained variance between the two.

The results achieved from the addition of these variables are dramatic relative to the previous equations, raising explanatory power significantly. The coefficient for output was further increased to about .58, indicating that every 1 percent of output growth generated nearly a .6 percent increase in labor productivity. It also showed service stations to be extraordinarily sensitive to changes in scale. For every 1 percent reduction in numbers, a 1.10 percent increase in productivity was achieved.

It is noteworthy, however, that no variable for establishment size for the other retailers was included in the equation. It was found that once the above variables were in place, the establishment variable for the remaining three retail types no longer contributed meaningfully to explaining the variance of P'. Its coefficient, although in the expected direction, was but .07 with a t-score of .4. This somewhat surprising result indicates that detectable gains from scale economies among the four types were confined to the service station sector.

Wages
The association of wages with output growth can be studied with three of the trades: food stores, car dealers, and department stores. While data are currently being compiled by the Bureau of Labor Statistics for service stations and restaurants, they do not span much of the time period for which the productivity statistics are available (Bureau of Labor Statistics 1979). Hence, these two retail types were excluded from this analysis.

F-tests for the regression incorporating dummy variables that gave the best results is significant at 5 percent from the no-difference model (not shown) and also exhausts the bulk of variance between the no-difference and complete-difference models, $F(4,45) = .88$.

$$P' = 20.15 + .4525\ 0' + .5168\ 0'_{fs} + .3379\ W' - .5020\ W'_{fs} \quad (7)$$
$$(1.2) \quad (6.3) \quad (2.9) \quad (2.1) \quad (2.9)$$
$$\text{Adj } R^2 = .55, \quad n = 54$$

The results, however, provide the surprising indication that wages in food stores are associated with negative productivity growth while just the opposite is true for auto dealers and department stores. Why such a distinction should arise is not clear. Wages for food stores, possibly under the impetus of strong union pressure, have risen somewhat more rapidly than retailing in general. But the differential is not large and gives no obvious basis for explaining the results obtained.

The results from the regression also indicate an interaction between the wages and output for food stores. With the wage variable in the equation, the dummy variable for food store output also enters significantly with a high positive coefficient. This compensated fully for the impact of the wage factor. The net effect was twofold. It suggested a stronger sensitivity to economic conditions for food stores than the other two retail types. It also indicated that after these adjustments, in a no-growth environment (including wages), food stores would nevertheless achieve a positive productivity change. It seems improbable, however, that food store unions would accept a new contract without provision for continuing higher wages.

CONCLUSIONS

The analysis of the relationship between output growth and productivity indicates that the entry of new technology into retailing depends heavily upon the rate at which the system is growing. The dependency appears greater than for manufacturing and may be increasing. With a forecast of slower real growth for the economy as a whole in the years ahead, the implication is that retailing's historic lag behind manufacturing in productivity growth may not only continue, but become more severe.

Despite the appearance of some differences, substantial similarity across the retail types studied appears with respect to the relationship between productivity and demand growth. Even the initial disparity discovered for gasoline stations disappeared when changes in establishment size were taken into consideration. This homogeneity was unexpected insofar as the capability for the various trades to introduce new technology under conditions of growth were believed dissimilar. Conceivably, with improved and more extensive data, some of the random noise in the data may be reduced and permit a finer search for such differences.

This homogeneity with respect to output growth raises an interesting question in regard to obvious difficulties faced by the restaurants in improving their efficiency. Here, output has been growing rapidly along with considerable technological ferment with the introduction of franchised fast food restaurants and their more automated operation and larger size. However, productivity growth has not been achieved and the inability for the trade to retain the benefits from new technology is disturbing.

Analysis of the role of economies of scale indicates, except again for gasoline stations, that little benefit to retail productivity emanates from this source. This finding is quite disappointing as more intensive utilization of existing retail resources is a logical place for deriving additional efficiency. It will be important to evaluate these results with cross-sectional empirical studies results that have shown benefits from fewer establishments per capita. Conceivably, productivity in time-series analysis may be affected adversely by the continuing growth of smaller establishments in many trades, such as restaurants. This may obscure real market-share shifts to larger places of business.

The differential effect of wages across the retail trades for which these data were available raises questions as to the role of this factor. While it is possible that the effects associated with higher wages in food stores may lead to lower productivity, this also is not a result obtained in cross-sectional research. Hence, either data quality or model specification errors may be at work. However, if such a negative effect is real for food stores, the regression results further indicate this trade to be far more reliant than others for growth, as a means of passing new technology, and that it is unique among the retail group.

In sum, while it is important to remember that the built-in association between productivity (output divided by input) and output may bias upward the coefficient of output growth, the results show that the retail system relies heavily upon economic growth as a means of lubricating technological change. Continuation of the slowdown in population and income growth, therefore, forecasts an extension of current limited progress in retail productivity. The discovery of new ways to extract better use of the resources in retailing, and means to diffuse these in a no-growth era, become important tasks for the future.

REFERENCES

Barger, H. (1955), Distribution's Place in the American Economy Since 1869, New York: National Bureau of Economic Research.

Bucklin, L. P. (1978), _Productivity in Marketing_, Chicago, IL:
American Marketing Association.

Bureau of Labor Statistics (1979), _Employment and Earnings,
United States 1909-1978_, Washington, DC: U.S. Department of
Labor.

_____ (1979), _Handbook of Labor Statistics, 1978_, Washington, DC: U.S. Department of Labor.

Controller's Congress (1963-1978), _Merchandising and Operating
Results_, New York: National Retail Merchants Association.

Cox, R., C. S. Goodman, and T. Fichandler (1965), _Distribution
in a High Level Economy_, Englewood Cliffs, NJ: Prentice-
Hall, Inc.

Kendrick, J. W. (1973), _Postwar Productivity Trends in the
United States, 1948-1967_, New York: Columbian University
Press, 112, 142.

Monthly Labor Review (1979), "Industry Output and Employment,
Bureau of Labor Statistics Projections to 1990" (April), 6-11.

Rao, P. and R. L. Miller (1971), _Applied Econometrics_, Belmont,
CA: Wadsworth Publishing Company, Inc., 149-152.

Schwartzman, D. (1971), _The Decline of Service in Retail Trade_,
Pullman, WA: Bureau of Economic and Business Research, Washington State University, 28, 44.

MANAGING THE RETAIL SALESFORCE

Gilbert A. Churchill, Jr., University of Wisconsin, Madison
Neil M. Ford, University of Wisconsin, Madison
Orville C. Walker, Jr., University of Minnesota, Minneapolis

ABSTRACT

This paper presents a conceptual framework that identifies
and integrates a number of variables which influence the performance of salespeople. This framework is used to evaluate
the existing research and current practices with respect to
sales management in retailing institutions. On the basis of
this evaluation, a number of promising areas for future research aimed at improving the effectiveness and efficiency of
the personal selling function in retailing are identified.

INTRODUCTION

Nearly 15 percent of the American workforce is employed
in retailing. While this sounds like an impressive fact, many
of today's retailers consider it an unfortunate state of affairs. The labor intensive nature of retailing is one reason
why retailing institutions have had great difficulty in improving their productivity. During the late 1960's and early
1970's annual productivity increases were lower in retailing
than in any other major sector in our economy. From 1968 to
1972, for instance, the average real output per man-hour increased an average of only 0.8 percent per year in retailing,
compared to 2.3 percent in manufacturing and 4.5 percent in
agriculture (McCammon and Hammer 1974). This, together with
increases in the legal minimum wage, has caused large increases
in the unit labor costs faced by retailers in recent years.

Many retailers have responded to these problems by reducing their labor forces - including sales personnel - to
"bare bones" levels. For example, one authority predicts that
more than half of all department store volume will be self-
service by the mid-1980's, compared with 40 percent self-
service volume in the mid-1970's (Bogart 1973).

A second response has been for retailers to attempt to
minimize the payroll and administrative costs associated with
the personnel they do employ. With respect to sales employees,
the prevailing attitude in retailing seems to be that such
people are little more than "order fillers" who should be
scraped from the dregs of the labor pool, provided with a

minimum possible amount of training, paid the prevailing mini- mum wage, and administered largely by staff specialists in the personnel department.

These attitudes are reflected in the personnel practices followed by many retailers, as discovered by one survey of 58 department stores in New York and California. In summarizing his findings, the researcher who conducted the survey concluded that:

> "The personnel department in the typical store seems subdued - characterized not only by a notable lack of enthusiasm or vitality but also by a deplorable absence of imagination. Its activities reflect mundane ap- proaches to such basic areas as recruitment, selection, training and compensation of those troops on the firing line - the salespeople in the store." (Burstiner 1976, pp. 13-14)

A number of researchers and writers have argued that this popular "cost minimization" approach to managing the personal selling function is myopic and may be self-defeating in the long-run. It stresses cost control while ignoring the po- tential impact of effective personal selling on sales volume and customer satisfaction (Cotham 1968).

There is also some evidence that many retail managers underestimate the importance their customers attach to the kind of service they receive from a store's salespeople. For ex- ample, one survey of both shoppers and retail managers in a Maryland shopping center found that 420 shoppers ranked "sales- clerk service" (availability, competence, congeniality, etc.) fourth in importance out of fourteen store patronage factors. However, retail managers responding in the same survey ranked salesclerk service much lower in importance, on the average, than did their customers (Jolson and Spath 1973).

OBJECTIVES

In view of the above criticisms of the prevailing atti- tudes toward personal selling in retailing today, it would seem appropriate for retailing managers and researchers to ob- jectively reevaluate the most appropriate role for personal selling to play in the promotional strategies of various types of stores and store departments. Similarly, the relative costs and benefits of implementing more sophisticated recruitment, selection, training and compensation practices for managing re- tail sales personnel should also be carefully considered.

35

The primary purpose of this paper, then, is to facilitate a systematic evaluation of current personnel attitudes and practices in retailing by presenting a conceptual framework which identifies and integrates a variety of factors which influence the performance of salespeople. This framework is used to examine existing research and current practices with respect to sales management in retailing institutions. Finally, on the basis of this examination, a number of unresolved issues are identified which may prove useful for guiding future theory development and empirical research aimed at improving the effectiveness and efficiency of the personal selling functions in retailing.

THE CONCEPTUAL FRAMEWORK

Performance

Prevailing literature in industrial and organizational psychology shows a worker's job performance is a function of five basic factors: (1) motivation, (2) aptitude, (3) skill level, (4) role perceptions or understanding of how the job should be done, and (5) personal, organizational and environmental variables which facilitate or inhibit performance. These factors are diagrammed in Figure 1, as part of an overall model of the determinants of a salesperson's performance.[1]

In most of the published literature the relationships among the various determinants of performance are viewed as multiplicative. The rationale for this is that if a worker is deficient in any one factor - such as aptitude or motivation - his or her performance is likely to be poor.

Rewards

The performance model outlined in Figure 1 shows that the salesperson's job performance affects the kinds and amounts of rewards he or she receives. This relationship between performance and rewards is very complex. For one thing, there are a number of different dimensions of sales performance that a

---

1. For a more detailed discussion of this model, its components, and the underlying conceptual and empirical literature in psychology and sales management, see O. C. Walker, Jr., G. A. Churchill, Jr., and N. M. Ford, "Where Do We Go From Here? Selected Conceptual and Empirical Issues Concerning The Motivation and Performance of the Industrial Salesforce," in Gerald Albaum and G. A. Churchill, Jr. (eds), Critical Issues in Sales Management: State-Of-The-Art and Future Research Needs. (Eugene, Oregon: College of Business Administration, University of Oregon, 1979), pp. 10-75.

retailer may or may not choose to evaluate and reward. A firm might evaluate its salespeople on total sales volume, departmental selling expenses, performance of stocking and administrative duties, or some combination of such performance dimensions.

FIGURE 1
THE MODEL -- DETERMINANTS OF SALESPERSON'S PERFORMANCE

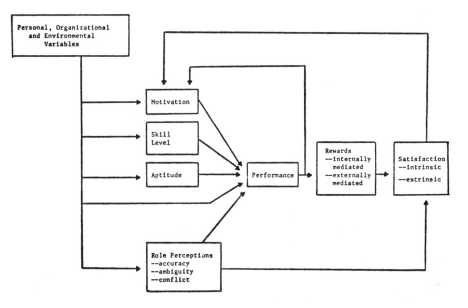

In addition to the multi-dimensional character of sales performance, there are also a variety of rewards that a store might bestow for any given level of performance. The model distinguishes between two broad types of rewards. Extrinsic rewards are those controlled and bestowed by people other than the salesperson, such as managers or customers. These rewards generally are related to lower-order human needs. They include things such as pay, financial incentives, security, recognition and promotion. Intrinsic rewards are those which salespeople largely attain for themselves and they relate to higher-order human needs. They include feelings of accomplishment, personal growth, and opportunities for career development.

As the model suggests, salespeople's perceptions of the kinds and amounts of rewards they will obtain in return for various types of job performance, together with the value they place on those rewards, strongly influence their motivation to perform.

Satisfaction

The rewards received by a salesperson have a major impact on his or her satisfaction with the job and the work environment. Once again, satisfaction is divided into two broad dimensions. Intrinsic satisfaction is related to the intrinsic rewards the salesperson obtains from the job, such as satisfaction with the work itself and with the opportunities for personal growth and accomplishment. Extrinsic satisfaction is related to the extrinsic rewards bestowed upon the salesperson such as satisfaction with pay, company policies, supervision, fellow workers, chances for promotion, and customers.

The amount of satisfaction salespeople obtain from their jobs is also influenced by their role perceptions. Salespeople who experience large amounts of conflict or uncertainty on the job tend to be less satisfied than those who do not.

Finally, the salesperson's level of job satisfaction is likely to have an impact on his or her motivation to perform. This relationship is explored more fully in the subsequent discussion of the motivation component of the model.

The Role of Perceptions Component

One of the most thoroughly researched determinants of sales performance in industrial sales situations is the salesperson's role perceptions. The role attached to the position of salesperson in any firm represents the set of activities or behaviors to be performed by any person occupying that position. This role is defined largely through the expectations, demands and pressures communicated to the salesperson by his or her role partners - people within and outside of the firm who have a vested interest in how the salesperson's job is performed, such as top management, supervisors, customers and family members. The salesperson's perceptions of these role partners' expectations and demands strongly influence his or her understanding of the job and of the kinds of behavior necessary to perform it well.

The role perceptions component of the total performance model is diagrammed in Figure 2. The major variables in this component are role accuracy, perceived role ambiguity and perceived role conflict.

Role accuracy refers to the degree to which the salesperson's perceptions of his or her role partners' demands - particularly those of company superiors - are accurate and correspond with what those role partners actually expect the salesperson to do when performing his or her job. Perceived role conflict arises when a salesperson believes that the demands of two or more role partners are incompatible and cannot

possibly be satisfied at the same time. Finally, <u>perceived
role ambiguity</u> occurs when salespeople feel they do not have
the information necessary to perform their jobs adequately.
They may be uncertain about what their role partners expect of
them in certain situations, how they should go about satisfying
those expectations, or how their performance will be evaluated
and rewarded.

FIGURE 2
THE ROLE PERCEPTIONS COMPONENT

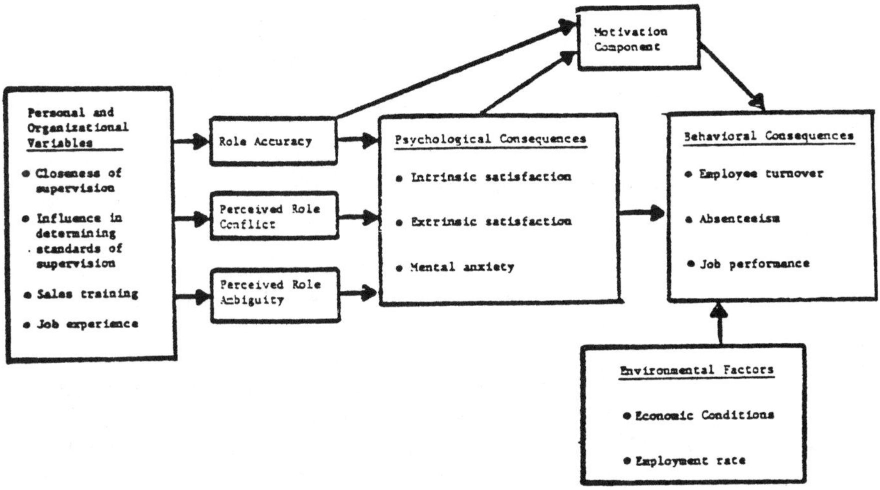

<u>Antecedents and consequences of role perceptions</u>. As
Figure 2 shows, the accuracy of salespeople's role perceptions
and the levels of role ambiguity and conflict they experience
are all influenced by a number of organizational variables and
personal characteristics. In the industrial selling literature, there is substantial empirical evidence that close supervision, employee participation in determining the standards by
which they are evaluated, performance feedback, sales training
and job experience are all negatively related to perceived role
ambiguity. Similarly, job experience and age have been found
to be negatively related to perceived role conflict. Unfortunately, the antecedents of role accuracy have not yet received
much empirical attention, though one would expect accuracy to
improve with closer supervision, greater influence in setting
standards, more frequent performance feedback, more sales
training and more job experience.

These three role perception variables have psychological
consequences for the individual salesperson. Perceptions of

role conflict and ambiguity are psychologically uncomfortable and stress-producing. Therefore, salespeople who experience high levels of conflict and ambiguity are likely to suffer more mental anxiety and be less satisfied with their jobs. Perceived role conflict is likely to have an especially negative effect on salespeople's satisfaction with the extrinsic aspects of their jobs. When salespeople face incompatible demands they may doubt their ability to satisfy the expectations of those who control external rewards, such as pay raises and promotions.

Perceived ambiguity, on the other hand, can have a negative effect on both intrinsic and extrinsic satisfaction. It is difficult for salespeople to like their jobs or achieve feelings of accomplishment and personal growth when they are uncertain about how they are expected to perform or how well they are performing. Similarly, such feelings of uncertainty can make salespeople pessimistic about their chances for promotion, future pay raises and other externally-mediated rewards.

Salespersons' role perceptions ultimately affect their behavior. Because role conflict and ambiguity can have a negative impact on salespeople's feelings of security and job satisfaction, they may lead to higher rates of absenteeism and turnover in the salesforce. But, this relationship is likely to be moderated somewhat by economic conditions and the availability of alternative jobs. In addition, a number of recent studies have investigated the impact of perceived role conflict and ambiguity on the salesperson's job performance. While there are some conflicting results, the majority of evidence indicates that conflict and ambiguity are negatively related to sales performance.

Role perceptions and retail sales performance. While the above statements concerning the relationships among role perceptions, employee satisfaction and job performance are based on substantial research in industrial sales settings, several parts of this component of the model have also received empirical support from several recent studies in retailing. While one of these studies focused primarily on department managers (Oliver and Brief 1977), two others examined the impact of role conflict and ambiguity on the satisfaction and performance of sales personnel in department stores (Donnelly and Etzel 1977; Dubinsky and Mattson 1979). These studies provide support for the proposition that both perceived role conflict and ambiguity have negative impacts on the satisfaction, organizational commitment and job performance of retail sales personnel.

To date, however, only Oliver and Brief have empirically examined the organizational factors and personnel characteristics related to the _amount_ of conflict and ambiguity experienced by store personnel, and their study focused on department managers rather than salespeople. Therefore, more empirical work is needed in order to understand the antecedents of role conflict and ambiguity among retail salespeople, and to devise managerial actions to reduce conflict and ambiguity and thereby improve salespeoples' morale and performance.

Aptitude and Skill Level Components

Aptitude. An individual's sales aptitude is typically viewed as the overall limit of, or constraint upon, a person's _ability_ to perform a sales job, given an adequate understanding of the role to be performed, motivation, learned skills and the absence of other external constraints. In other words, two people with equal motivation, role perceptions and skills might perform at very different levels simply because one has more aptitude or ability than the other.

A number of personal and psychological characteristics are thought to be related to, or determinants of, sales ability. These characteristics include:

1) _physical factors_, such as age, sex, height, and physical attractiveness;
2) _mental abilities_, such as verbal intelligence, mathematical ability, educational attainment, and previous sales experience;
3) _personality characteristics_, such as empathy, ego strength, sociability, aggressiveness and dominance.

Numerous studies have attempted to predict variations in sales performance by measuring one or more of these aptitude-related personal variables. While many such studies have found statistically significant relationships between aptitude variables and performance, however, such broad measures of aptitude by themselves generally have not been able to explain a very large proportion of the variance in sales performance in industrial selling; nor have they been capable of predicting the future sales success of individuals across different types of selling jobs in different companies.

Sales aptitude and employee selection in retailing. A number of published studies have attempted to identify personal characteristics related to sales aptitude - and ultimately to sales performance - in retailing. Most of these studies, however, have focused on physical factors and experience rather than on the mental or personality characteristics of successful retail salespeople (French 1960; Cotham 1969; Weaver 1969; Churchill, Collins and Strang 1975; Spivey, Munson and Locander 1979). This orientation is also apparent in the salesperson selection practices of many retail personnel departments. One recent survey reports that while 72 percent of the stores studied used application blanks and 89 percent checked the references of prospective sales employees, more than two-thirds of the responding stores did no testing to determine applicants' mental abilities or personality traits (Burstiner 1976, pp. 6-10).

As with the research in industrial selling, studies of aptitude and sales ability in retail settings have produced inconsistent results. Some studies have found that personal characteristics such as age, education and past sales experience are strongly related to salesclerks' subsequent sales performance, but other studies have found no significant relationship between such personal characteristics and performance. One plausible explanation for the lack of consistent relationships between personal characteristics and sales success is that different types of sales jobs require salespeople to perform different activities and to deal with different types of customers. Thus, people with particular traits and abilities may have the aptitude necessary for success in some sales jobs and in dealing with some types of customers, but not others. This suggests that it may be futile to look for a single "type" of person who is most likely to be successful in all kinds of retail selling jobs. Instead, managers and researchers should try to identify those specific characteristics and abilities that enable a salesperson to handle the unique selling tasks and problems faced in different types of sales jobs. This would necessitate (1) the development of a taxonomy of retail sales jobs based on variations in customer types, product characteristics and selling activities; and (2) research leading to a "contingency" theory of sales aptitude which would identify those personal characteristics related to success in a particular type of retail sales job. Some preliminary work on a contingency approach to salesforce selection is currently underway in the industrial sales literature, but no similar work has as yet been undertaken in retailing (Weitz 1979).

Skill level. Skill level refers to a salesperson's learned proficiency at performing the tasks associated with his or her job. While aptitude and skill level are related constructs, aptitude consists of a set of relatively enduring personal abilities while skills are proficiency levels at performing specific tasks which can change rapidly with learning and experience.

The skills needed for good sales performance include

(1) <u>salesmanship skills</u>, such as knowing how to present product information, how to close a sale, how to suggest related purchases, etc.; (2) <u>interpersonal skills</u>, such as knowing how to cope with and resolve conflicts; and (3) <u>technical skills</u>, such as knowledge of product features and benefits and the procedural skills required by store policies.

<u>Selling skills and sales training in retailing</u>. Many textbooks have attempted to describe salesmanship skills, but no one has yet developed a detailed inventory of the other kinds of skills involved in either retail or industrial selling. Since it is likely that <u>different</u> kinds of skills are needed for performing various types of selling tasks in different selling situations, the development of a taxonomy of selling skills is a worthwhile conceptual goal.

Obviously, the salesperson's past selling experience and the extensiveness and content of the store's sales training program both affect the individual's skill level. It is clear, however, that retailers are much less concerned with the development of selling skills than other marketing organizations. While industrial goods manufacturers spend an average of $19,000 per salesperson on training, and consumer goods manufacturers spend over $13,000 (<u>Sales and Marketing Management</u> 1980, p. 67), the average department store devotes only 12.5 hours to training a new salesclerk; 6 hours of which are spent explaining the store's registers, systems and policies (Burstiner 1976, pp. 11-12).

Regardless of the amount of time and money devoted to sales training in various kinds of marketing organizations, however, there is an almost complete vacuum of published knowledge concerning the effects of these training programs on salespersons' skills, behavior and performance. While there are a number of articles on training in the sales and retailing literature, they are typically how-to-do-it or experiential pieces. Few past studies have attempted to evaluate the psychological or behavioral effects of alternative training methods (Catalenello and Kirkpatrick 1968). This would seem to be a fruitful area for research.

The Motivation Component

In recent years most industrial and organizational psychologists have come to view "motivation" as a general label for the determinants of (a) the choice to initiate effort on a certain task, (b) the choice to expend a certain amount of effort on that task, and (c) the choice to persist in expending effort over a period of time. Here <u>motivation</u> is viewed as <u>the amount of effort a salesperson desires to expend on each of the activities or tasks associated with his or her job</u>.

An expectancy model of motivation, adopted to a selling context, is diagrammed in Figure 3. The model views motivation as the amount of effort the salesperson desires to expend on a particular task (i) associated with his or her job. It assumes that expending effort on a variety of such tasks will lead to some level of achievement on one or more dimensions of job performance (j), such as total sales volume, increased sales of "special" items, or the reduction of register errors. It is further assumed that the salesperson's performance on at least some of these dimensions will be evaluated by his or her superiors and rewarded with one or more of a variety of rewards (k). These might be externally mediated rewards controlled by the salesperson's superiors, such as increased pay, recognition or a promotion, or they might be internally mediated rewards, such as feelings of accomplishment or personal growth. A salesperson's motivation to expend effort on a given task, then, is determined by three sets of perceptions: (1) expectancies, (2) instrumentalities, and (3) valence for rewards.

FIGURE 3
THE MOTIVATION COMPONENT

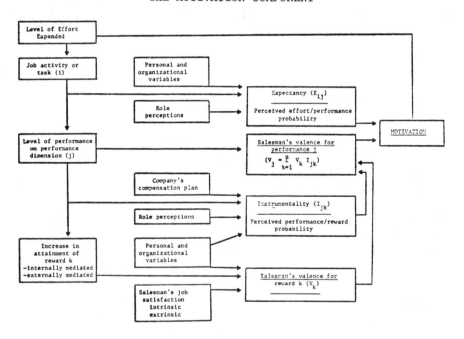

Expectancy (E_{ij}). Expectancies are the salesperson's perceptions of the <u>linkages between effort and job performance</u>. Specifically, an expectancy is the salesperson's estimate of the probability that expending a given amount of effort on task (i) will lead to an improved level of performance on some performance dimension (j).

Instrumentality (I_{jk}). Instrumentalities are the salesperson's perceptions of the <u>linkages between job performance and the various rewards he or she will receive</u>. An instrumentality, then, is the degree to which a salesperson believes an improved level of performance on performance dimension (j) will lead to the increased attainment of a particular reward (k).

Valence for rewards (V_k). Valence for rewards is the salesperson's perception of the <u>desirability of receiving an increased amount of reward (k)</u> that he or she might attain as a result of improved performance.

The sales motivation model outlined in Figure 3 predicts the level of a salesperson's motivation to expend effort on a specific job activity (i) by multiplying the individual's expectancies that the activity will lead to given levels of performance on various dimensions times his or her valence for these levels of performance, and then summing across all performance dimensions. Symbolically:

$$F_i = \sum_{j=1}^{p} E_{ij} V_j \qquad \begin{array}{l} i = 1, \ldots, a \\[1em] j = 1, \ldots, p \end{array}$$

where:

F_i = the force on the individual to perform activity i;

E_{ij} = the expectancy that activity i will lead to performance j;

V_j = the valence of performance outcome j;

a = the number of job activities;

p = the number of performance dimensions.

The salesperson's valence for a particular performance outcome (V_j), in turn, is predicted by his or her perception of the instrumentality of improved performance on dimension j for attaining various rewards multiplied by the valence of those rewards for the individual, summed across all relevant rewards. Symbolically:

$$V_j = \sum_{k=1}^{r} I_{jk} V_k .$$

$$j = 1, \ldots, p$$

$$k = 1, \ldots, r$$

where:

V_j = the salesman's valence for performance outcome j;

I_{jk} = the salesman's perception of the instrumentality of outcome j for the attainment of reward k;

V_k = the salesman's valence for reward k;

p = the number of performance dimensions;

r = the number of rewards.

Motivation in retail selling. The motivation model discussed above has been extensively tested, although only two studies have been undertaken with sales employees (Oliver 1974; Churchill, Ford and Walker 1978). Since motivation is only one of several determinants of job performance, an expectancy model of motivation by itself is not appropriate for predicting a worker's performance, even though many researchers have attempted to do so. In such studies, workers' $E(\Sigma IV)$ scores are correlated across subjects with measures of actual performance, determined either objectively or by superior, peer or self-ratings. Most of these studies report positive results, with r^2's ranging from .01 to .41.

To date, no published studies have employed a motivation model like the one above to investigate the motivation and performance of retail salesclerks. Indeed, there have been virtually no published studies dealing with any aspect of the compensation or motivation of retail sales personnel.

This lack of research on retail sales motivation is reflected in the current compensation practices of many retail organizations. A survey of 52 department stores found that over two-thirds compensated their salespeople with straight salary, and only 17 percent offered any form of financial incentives tied to actual job performance (Burstiner 1976, p. 13).

Obviously, then, there are many unanswered questions concerning the most effective types of rewards to use in motivating retail salespeople and the most appropriate means for linking the attainment of those rewards to specific aspects of job performance. Such questions represent fertile ground for future research and management action.

The Personal, Organizational and Environmental Variables Component

Figure 1 suggests that personal, organizational and environmental variables influence sales performance in two ways: (1) through interactions with other performance determinants, such as role perceptions and motivation; and (2) by directly facilitating or constraining the individual's ability to perform his or her job. As we have seen, personal and organizational variables - such as job experience and closeness of supervision - have been found to be related to the amount of role conflict and ambiguity experienced by salespeople in both industrial and retail situations. In addition, one study has found that personal characteristics are related to motivation in the sense that industrial salespeople's valences for various job-related rewards (e.g., pay, promotion, etc.) differ with age, education and family size (Churchill, Ford and Walker 1979). No such studies have been done, however, among retail sales employees.

Several published studies have related a number of organizational and environmental factors directly to variations in sales performance in industrial settings. These studies have found statistically significant relationships between performance and organizational factors such as company advertising expenditures, the firm's current market share and closeness of supervision within the salesforce. Similarly, many of the same studies have found performance to be related to environmental factors like territory potential, concentration of customers, the salesperson's workload and the intensity of competition. Once again, however, no published research has examined the impact of environmental or organizational factors on sales productivity across stores or across departments within a store. The existence of such influences, though, would have implications for determining the most appropriate procedures and criteria to use when evaluating the performance and productivity of a store's sales employees. Simple sales volume or selling-expense-as-a-percentage-of-sales criteria may be inappropriate if environmental or organizational variables beyond the salesperson's control are responsible for causing differences in productivity across departments.

CONCLUSIONS

In view of the existing theory and research regarding the determinants of sales performance found in the industrial psychology and sales management literature, both the available body of empirical knowledge and the current personnel management practices in retailing appear to be underdeveloped. This brief review has identified a number of unresolved issues which

47

represent promising areas for future research and for the development of management practices aimed at improving the productivity and efficiency of retail sales personnel. The following list summarizes some of these issues.

- WHAT PERSONAL AND ORGANIZATIONAL VARIABLES AFFECT THE AMOUNT OF ROLE CONFLICT AND AMBIGUITY EXPERIENCED BY SALESCLERKS? WHAT ACTIONS CAN MANAGEMENT TAKE TO REDUCE PERCEIVED CONFLICT AND AMBIGUITY AND THEREBY IMPROVE THE SATISFACTION, ORGANIZATIONAL COMMITMENT AND PERFORMANCE OF SALES PERSONNEL?

- WHAT PERSONAL CHARACTERISTICS INFLUENCE A PERSON'S ABILITY TO SELL SPECIFIC TYPES OF PRODUCTS TO SPECIFIC TYPES OF CUSTOMERS? CAN A "CONTINGENCY" THEORY OF SALES APTITUDE BE DEVELOPED TO GUIDE THE DEVELOPMENT OF IMPROVED SELECTION PROCEDURES?

- HOW DO ALTERNATIVE SALES TRAINING METHODS AND PROCEDURES AFFECT THE ULTIMATE BEHAVIOR AND PERFORMANCE OF RETAIL SALESPEOPLE?

- WHAT TYPES OF REWARDS ARE MOST EFFECTIVE FOR MOTIVATING RETAIL SALES PERSONNEL? DO SALESCLERKS WITH DIFFERENT PERSONAL CHARACTERISTICS DESIRE DIFFERENT TYPES OF REWARDS? WHAT COMPENSATION METHODS ARE MOST EFFECTIVE FOR MOTIVATING SPECIFIC TYPES OF BEHAVIOR AND PERFORMANCE AMONG MEMBERS OF THE RETAIL SALESFORCE?

- HOW DO ENVIRONMENTAL AND ORGANIZATIONAL FACTORS AFFECT SALES PERFORMANCE ACROSS SALESCLERKS AND DEPARTMENTS? HOW CAN THE IMPACT OF SUCH "NON-CONTROLLABLE" FACTORS BE TAKEN INTO ACCOUNT IN EVALUATING THE PERFORMANCE OF INDIVIDUAL SALESCLERKS?

Finally, it should be apparent that the conceptual framework discussed above recognizes that the kinds of tasks and activities associated with a particular sales job - and therefore the requirements for successful job performance - vary according to the type of product to be sold, the kinds of customers in the target market, and the characteristics of the organization and its environment. This implies that no single personal selling strategy, nor set of personnel practices, is appropriate for all selling situations. Consequently, a great deal more thought should be given to the most appropriate role for personal selling to play within different departments or organizational units of a retail organization, and to the kinds of personnel practices necessary to motivate and direct salesclerks in different kinds of selling situations. This is particularly true in light of the fact that many larger department stores have embraced the principles of market segmentation and are adjusting the merchandising and marketing practices of various departments to appeal to distinct and different customer groups. Minimizing sales personnel, and the costs associated with compensating and managing them, is undoubtedly the correct approach for some departments and some types of stores appealing to certain segments of the market. But a philosophy of improving the competence and motivation of salesclerks may well pay dividends in the form of increased revenues, reduced turnover and improved customer satisfaction in other types of stores and departments.

REFERENCES

Bogart, Leo (1973), "The Future of Retailing," Harvard Business Review, 51 (November-December), 16-32.

Burstiner, Irving (1976), "Current Personnel Practices in Department Stores," Journal of Retailing, 51 (Winter), 6-14.

Catalenello, R. F., and D. L. Kirkpatrick (1968), "Evaluating Training Programs: The State of the Art," Training and Development Journal, 21 (May), 2-9.

Churchill, G. A., Jr., R. H. Collins, and W. A. Strang (1975), "Should Retail Salespersons be Similar to Their Customers?" Journal of Retailing, 51 (Fall), 29-42.

_____, N. M. Ford, and O. C. Walker, Jr. (1978), "Predicting a Salesperson's Job Effort and Performance: Theoretical, Empirical and Methodological Considerations," paper presented at the AMA/MSI Sales Management Workshop, Cambridge, MA.

_____ (1979), "Personal Characteristics of Salespeople and the Attractiveness of Alternative Rewards," Journal of Business Research, 7, 25-50.

Cotham, James C., III (1968), "The Case for Personal Selling: Some Retailing Myths Exploded," Business Horizons, 11 (April), 75-81.

_____ (1969), "Using Personal History Information in Retail Salesman Selection," Journal of Retailing, 45 (Spring), 31-38.

Donnelly, J. H., and M. J. Etzel (1977), "Retail Store Performance and Job Satisfaction," Journal of Retailing, 53 (Summer), 23-28.

Dubinsky, A. J., and B. E. Mattson (1979), "Consequences of Role Conflict and Ambiguity Experienced by Retail Salespeople," Journal of Retailing, 55 (Winter), 70-86.

French, C. L. (1960), "Correlates of Success in Retail Selling," American Journal of Sociology, 66, 128-134.

Jolson, M. A., and W. F. Spath (1973), "Understanding and Fulfilling Shoppers' Requirements: An Anomaly in Retailing," Journal of Retailing, 49 (Summer), 38-46.

McCammon, B. C., Jr., and W. L. Hammer (1974), "A Frame of Reference for Improving Productivity in Distribution," Atlanta Economic Review, 24 (September-October).

Oliver, R. L. (1974), "Expectancy Theory Predictions of Salesmen's Performance," Journal of Marketing Research, 11 (August), 243-253.

_____, and A. P. Brief (1977), "Determinants and Consequences of Role Conflict and Ambiguity Among Retail Sales Managers," Journal of Retailing, 53 (Winter), 47-58.

Sales and Marketing Management (1980), "Survey of Selling Costs" (February 25).

Spivey, W. A., J. M. Munson, and W. B. Locander (1979), "Meeting Retail Staffing Needs Via Improved Selection," Journal of Retailing, 55 (Winter).

Weaver, C. N. (1969), "An Empirical Study to Aid in the Selection of Retail Salesclerks," Journal of Retailing, 45, 22-26.

Weitz, B. A. (1979), "A Critical Review of Personal Selling Research: The Need for Contingency Approaches," in Critical Issues in Sales Management: State-of-the-Art and Future Research Needs, G. Albaum and G. A. Churchill, Jr., eds. Eugene, Oregon: University of Oregon, 107-120.

PORTFOLIO THEORY AND THE RETAILING LIFE CYCLE

William R. Davidson, Management Horizons, Inc., Columbus
Nancy E. Johnson, Management Horizons, Inc., Columbus

Continuing with the concept of life cycle management as it relates to retailing that we first discussed at this workshop in 1979, we want to show how the multiplicity of life cycles that any one store, or department, may have at any one given time, can be managed into a portfolio of assets to help maximize the goals of the organization. Further, when life cycles are extended to the total store level, they can be combined with the life cycles of other stores to create a portfolio of life cycles at varying stages to both hedge against the ill-effects of any one downturn and to always be growing at some point. When this portfolio is managed efficiently and assets transferred to the point where they can be utilized most effectively, the store or corporation can maximize its wealth.

THE LIFE CYCLES WITHIN A RETAILING OPERATION

Any merchandise supplier, merchandise classification, department, division, location or store is at some point on the life cycle. Within even one classification, there may be two new, untested items, three "hot" items, two items whose sales have peaked yet maintain an acceptable level of sales, and one item that is a candidate for deletion. Each carries with it its own set of customers. (See Exhibit One).

A store is simply a composite of life cycles with each component moving at its own pace and scale. So, too, are individual stores moving along their own life cycles. Within one retailing organization, individual stores can be found in each part of the life cycle. An example of this is K Mart. Here, in the early years, most individual stores were in the stage of increasing profitability based on a concept of a five-year period to achieve maximum profitability. From 1971-1976, the number of K Mart stores in the "increasing profitability" cycle kept increasing owing to rapid store openings.

However, the number of store units and the amount of store square footage already in the "increasing profitability" stage was declining almost every year after 1971. This should be an indication to management of approaching maturity.

As we know from previous life cycle discussions, stores

(or any item or product) in the maturity stage face declining
market share and a drop in profits (Davidson, Bates and Bass,
1976). In 1971, K Mart had 486 units with 31.4 million square
feet of total space, 70% of which was in the "increasing profitability stage." By 1976, there were 1,206 units with a total
of 746 million square feet of space, only 58% of which was in
the "increasing profitability stage." In the case of K Mart,
finding the portfolio of stores weighted in favor of maturing
stores should be the signal for a new phase of the life cycle--
growth renewal--to ward off the pending decline phase.

The same example can apply to any supplier with regard to
his product line. While items that are basic to his line may
long ago have reached the maturity or decline stage, the total
line can become increasingly profitable by keeping a larger
share of the line in the growth and "increasing profitability"
stage to make up for the declining profits on the basics.

A buyer should examine his department in this way by merchandise line to keep the total department in the growth stage.
Once a department slips into the maturity stage, profits may
not be as strong as before, market share may stagnate or
decline, and the department will face loss of primary space or
a drop in total square footage, inventory investment, or personnel to a growth department. Without a growth renewal strategy, regaining what has been lost would be an irrational decision by management.

Instituting a growth renewal strategy, however, can become
unfeasible due to the structure of the retailing accounting
cycle (a strict fiscal year reporting system with six month
seasonal financing budgets). A financing plan for a department
is often only formally laid out for six months to a year. However, funding a new department to the "increasing profitability" stage or a maturing department through a successful growth
renewal may take longer or shorter than a conventional retailing accounting cycle. The ideal would be to put a department
or division on a "life cycle" accounting cycle -- made flexible
by the individual needs and goals of that department. Thus,
funding would not risk cutting at a crucial point in the introduction stage because immediate goals had not been reached.

PORTFOLIO MANAGEMENT IN THEORY

Risk and return are the two key elements in portfolio management. Success or failure is determined by how these two are
combined for the particular assets (i.e., capital, inventory,
space, personnel) in a portfolio.

52

There are two forms of risk:

1. Diversifiable (unsystematic) risk is the financial risk relating to the uncertain profitability of individual companies, departments or individual merchandise classifications.

2. Non-diversifiable (systematic) risk is the market risk relating to the economic and psychological factors affecting the entire market.

To construct a rational portfolio of stores, departments, locations or merchandise classifications, a manager must be able to answer:

- Which particular "package" of "investments" should be chosen for the given risk portion of the portfolio?

- How should the portfolio investment, however defined, be divided up among the possibilities in that form of investment (giving different weights to the various "investments")?

- How should the portfolio be leveraged (internal growth or debt)?

There are six basic assumptions that underlie all portfolio analysis:

- The rate of return is the most important outcome of any investment.

- Investors visualize the various possible rates of return from any asset in a probabilistic fashion.

- Investors define risk as the variability of return and are willing to base their investment decision on only two things—expected return and risk.

- Investors prefer to hold the investment with the maximum rate of return in any given risk class they select, or conversely, investors prefer to minimize risk at whatever expected rate of return they seek.

- Of the three goals that an investor can have, wealth maximization is more rational than high income or high price appreciation.

- Rational investors will diversify their holdings
  across industries, types of store, department, or
  merchandise classification in order to avoid the
  downside aspects of diversifiable risks.

EXAMPLES OF PORTFOLIO THEORY IN VARIOUS
LEVELS OF RETAILING MANAGEMENT

Portfolio theory can be applied to retailing at all decision making levels. We have provided four examples to show its
use today in four different situations.

CASE EXAMPLE[1]

LAZARUS, a Columbus, Ohio, division of Federated Department
Stores, exemplifies a complex set of situations relating to the
portfolio within the existing organization.

The problems of portfolio management, as related to the
retail life cycle, are no more complex in any type of institution than in the large full-service conventional department
store company with a complete range of merchandise categories
normally sold in such stores. For many years, Lazarus enjoyed
a dominant market position in the greater metropolitan area of
Columbus. The downtown store was a full line operation, with
180 merchandise departments selling over 1200 merchandise classifications, and offering the complete range of department
store services normally associated with institutions such as
Marshall Field, Jordan Marsh, Hudson's, Rich's, The Emporium,
etc.

Because of the large size and dominance of the downtown
store, and the ease of accessibility of the downtown area in
Columbus from all parts of the metropolitan area, Lazarus was
late in going to the suburbs, compared with many other conventional department store organizations, especially in much
larger cities. With the tremendous growth of suburban shopping
centers and free-standing general merchandise and specialty
mass merchandising establishments in the rapidly growing Columbus area during the 1960's and early 1970's, Lazarus experienced

---

1. The material is based primarily upon a Harvard Business
School case, Lazarus Company, prepared by Lynda Diane Baydin
under the direction of Professor Walter J. Salmon, and distrib-
uted by the Intercollegiate Case Clearing House, Soldiers Field,
Boston, Massachusetts. It is supplemented to a minor extent by
MH local observations of Columbus and Indianapolis Lazarus Stores.

some decline in total market share and in profitability. In addition to tracking total market share, Lazarus also estimated trends in market share by individual departments and carefully monitored, by department, major competition. The erosion of market share was much more serious among certain "problem" departments than for the company as a whole. Some executives felt that the long history of Lazarus mandated a complete range of departments in order to attract customers to Lazarus. The problem was especially severe because many of the newer forms of competition for these problem departments had a much lower expense structure than that of a full service traditional department store, and could operate profitably at lower markups than required to achieve profitability than was the case with conventional department stores.

Any visitor to a group of Lazarus establishments would infer that Lazarus decided to maintain a full range of department store merchandise classifications and services in its major Columbus stores where there is a long history of consumer expectancy that all such products and services are available. Another inference from such visits is that the decision was to the effect that the same portfolio is not a requirement for each location. Exhibit Two, showing three of the problem areas, dramatizes the importance of portfolio management, by indicating that the competitive situation for any component of a company's portfolio may be vastly different from that of others, and may be suggestive that some components of the portfolio are in different phases of the life cycle than others, calling either for imaginative growth renewal strategies, de-emphasis, or possible termination.

CASE EXAMPLE[2]

DAYTON-HUDSON CORPORATION, a Minneapolis headquartered free form of diversified retailing corporation, operates in 44 states through department stores, low-margin stores and specialty stores. Additionally, through its former real estate business, it also owned, developed and managed regional shopping centers and other properties. It illustrates a changing portfolio achieved both by internal growth and by acquisition.

Since 1970, Dayton-Hudson Corporation has grown from 95 stores in 18 states to 588 stores in 44 states. It has moved

---

2. The material in this case example has been prepared on the basis of 10-K reports submitted to the Security and Exchange Commission, corporate annual reports, and miscellaneous press comments.

up from fourteenth largest to seventh largest among the
nation's non-food retailers. Total retail space has grown by
92%; revenues have grown by 177%; earnings have grown by 1,296%.

Dayton-Hudson notes that the key to the company's growth
has been balance between: (1) traditional department store and
shopping center places and major ventures into low-margin and
specialty store retailing; (2) acquisitions and internally
developed strategies; (3) internal and external sources of
funds; (4) operating company autonomy and corporate direction;
and (5) long-term return and long-term profitability.

As far as their three retailing divisions are concerned,
each group represents a distinctly different approach to the
consumer. All three reflect a unifying merchandising philosophy and emphasize dominant selections, quality, fashion
and value.

The department store group is made up of five operating
companies, each emphasizing fashion leadership, quality merchandise, broad selections and customer service. They are the
J.L. Hudson Corporation in Michigan and Ohio, Dayton's in
Minnesota and North Dakota, Diamond's in Arizona and Nevada,
Lipman's in Oregon, and Brown's in Oklahoma. The entire
department store division was operating a total of 51 stores
at year end, most located in strong regional shopping centers.

The low-margin division is comprised of two distinct
strategies: Target is a low-margin department store chain
operating 67 stores in ten mid-western and southeastern states.
In basic merchandise Target concentrates on quality name brand
goods. Target's 23% increase in revenues in 1978 widened its
lead as the corporation's largest revenue producer. Lechmere
is a Boston based hardlines retailer with a long-standing reputation as a market leader in competitive pricing of big ticket
items. It operates six stores in Massachusetts and New Hamp-
shire.

The specialty store group consisted in 1978 of three multi-
store companies: B. Dalton Bookseller, a national chain operating 357 bookstores; Dayton-Hudson Jeweler, a group of six
regional fine jewelry retailers; and Team, a chain of owned and
franchised consumer electronics stores.[3] B. Dalton sells books

_____

3. Still, in 1978, management reached the decision to sell
Team because its business strategy was not compatible with the
Corporation's aggressive retail growth plans. Instead, assets
will be invested in the three fastest growing divisions: Target,
Mervyn's and B. Dalton.

in a way that is as modern as the computer, a tool it has used to add speed and efficiency to the art of bringing readers and books together. In 1977, B. Dalton sold more hard cover books than any other retailer in the U.S.

Dayton-Hudson Corporation's primary financial objective is to provide the shareholders with an optimum return on investment over time. Specific goals are to earn a consistent return on shareholders' equity of at least 14% and sustain an annual growth in earnings per share of common stock of at least 10%. In 1978, return on beginning-of-year common shareholders' equity was 28.5%. Earnings per share have increased at a compound annual growth rate of 20% since 1971 and 11% since 1966.

Each of Dayton-Hudson's projects are expected to achieve an ROI of at least 12% by the fifth year of operation, and an internal rate of return with discounted cash flow of at least 10% over the life of the project. These standards are achievable by each of their retailing businesses despite differences in return on sales. For example, a department store will produce a higher return on sales than a low-margin store but will require more assets than a low-margin store to achieve a given sales level. Certain strategies have maintained a higher return or reach a satisfactory level of return sooner than others, thereby justifying a faster rate of expansion.

Early in 1978, Dayton-Hudson announced an agreement in principle to acquire Mervyn's, a fast growing West Coast chain of 42 highly centralized and systematized soft goods department stores. Mervyn's is a highly promotional organization, featuring much private brand merchandise or products manufactured to its own specifications. Most observers view Mervyn's as strongly positioned between the price/value, service, and fashion appeal of conventional department stores and discount department stores. Thus, it adds a new dimension to the Dayton-Hudson portfolio. At the end of the first quarter of 1979, Lipman's operations were discontinued and the stores sold, again changing the Dayton-Hudson portfolio. Some of the assets were added to Mervyn's operations.

Exhibit Three illustrates the dynamic portfolio of Dayton-Hudson, and the sales impact of the Mervyn acquisition, when consolidated with 1978 corporate sales.

HART, SCHAFFNER & MARX, a New York based corporation known for its apparel manufacturing division, also owns and operates 274 clothing stores across the country. It shows that a successful dual distribution system can be established. Dual distribution was once a point of fact in the tailored clothing industry. However, the manufacturers tended to view the retail operation as an outlet/warehouse for their manufacturing instead of as a profit center. The one manufacturer to buck this trend is H.S. & M., which has grown their retail operation into a $350 million business.

Each set of stores is viewed as a part of the total retail portfolio and performance is judged by its role as a profit center. Thus, the mix of their retail portfolio has changed over the years as different types of retailers or merchandise mixes become more appealing to the consumer and bottom line.[5]

Now that H.S. & M. has established a strong level of competency in a narrowly defined retail market (classic quality menswear stores), they are expanding their customer base by appealing to younger, fashion-conscious and value-oriented customers, both men and women. Two different marketing strategies were used to keep existing stores in either the "increasing profitability" or mature stage in their own life cycles.

First, major emphasis has been placed in merchandising on lowering starting price points and introducing new clothing and sportswear directions. Second, many of the mature, older and more profitable stores were remodeled to improve the initial impact of the stores to potential customers. The success of this effort in 1979 has encouraged H.S. & M. to put another $4 million into growth renewal for 1980.

---

4. The material in this case example has been prepared on the basis of 10-K reports submitted to the Security & Exchange Commission, corporate annual reports and miscellaneous press comments.

5. For the past five years, retailing has provided 60-65% of all H.S. & M. sales. Their largest retailing units include Silverwoods (19 stores), Baskin (24), Chas. A. Stevens (20), Wallachs (26), R. J. Boggs (9), Zachry (9), James K. Wilson (11), Leopold Price & Rolle (10) and Hastings (14).

CASE EXAMPLE[6]

GENERAL MILLS, the Minneapolis based international corporation, has successfully extended its portfolio beyond food processing into specialty retailing and other areas to diversify its portfolio of assets to minimize both systematic and unsystematic risk.

The $3.7 billion a year corporation is actually a diversified portfolio of consumer goods and services that includes creative products (like Kenner & Parker Brothers games and toys), restaurants (York Steak House and Red Lobster), fashion manufacturing (David Crystal, Ship & Shore, and Monet Jewelry) and specialty retailing (see list in Exhibit Four).

For the past few years, General Mills has been active in all five of their business units. It is a part of their corporate strategy to regularly assess the deployment of their assets along with other performance goals. The major emphasis of the strategy is on leadership in the marketing of these areas of consumer goods and services through internal growth. Since 1976, General Mills has supported this strategy with an average 21% annual increase in fixed asset investments.

While the largest single share of this increase is devoted to the food business (40%), 15% is directed toward specialty retailing (33 new outlets were planned in 1979). This portfolio was strong enough to have all of its growth financed internally.

In an effort to keep this strong position, in 1979 General Mills closed its Kimberly women's sportswear business, sold the Smiths Food Group (U.K.) and the Intraworld travel business. This reduced the number of business units to the current five. These five will be the center of activity for the near future.

THE FUTURE OF PORTFOLIO THEORY IN RETAILING

When portfolio analysis is combined with life cycle management and basic income statement analysis for any given department, merchandise category or location, it adds to the analysis that can be done by a store to aid in planning with wealth maximization goals. It helps manage a constantly changing mix of

---

6. The material in this case example has been prepared on the basis of 10-K reports submitted to the Security & Exchange Commission, corporate annual reports, and miscellaneous press comments.

merchandise and locational strategies. The expansion or death of classifications can be made evident, and also the need for flexibility by season.

Externally, portfolio analysis can also have a substantial impact on a retailing establishment. No retailer is too large or too small to: (1) be considered for acquisition or divestiture, or (2) be impacted by the acquisition or divestiture of someone else. (Exhibit Five).

Either you are a Rich's adjusting to being bought by a Federated, or you are an Abraham & Strauss feeling the impact of another large store joining the corporation. Anyone located in a mall or strip shopping center may find that, overnight, the dollar power of a major corporation has moved next door -- yet nothing physically has changed.

In a matter of days, an acquisition or divestiture can change the situation for not only internal management but also the competition and suppliers. A new owner may have vastly different plans for a store than the former owners did, greatly changing the nature of competition in a given trading area. Suppliers, too, may find themselves dealing with a completely different kind of customer when a store changes hands.

Any corporation that intends to keep itself in the "increasing profitability" stage of its life cycle must be looking for ways to improve--either internally or through acquisition. If the corporation is multi-dimensional in income sources (it is making or selling more than one kind of widget), then it should have a dynamic portfolio of assets--and a shopping list. The key is to remember that the door of portfolio management swings both ways, however. What is acquirable is also expandable.

REFERENCES

Davidson, William R., Albert D. Bates, & Stephen J. Bass (1976), "The Retail Life Cycle," Harvard Business Review, (November-December), pp. 89-96.

Davidson, William R. and John E. Smallwood (1980), "An Overview of Management of the Retail Life Cycle," Competitive Structure in Retail Markets: The Department Store Perspective, American Marketing Association.

Francis, Jack Clark, Investments: Analysis & Management, New York; McGraw-Hill, 1976.

Latane, Henry and Donald L. Tuttle, Security Analysis & Portfolio Management, New York: Ronald Press, 1975.

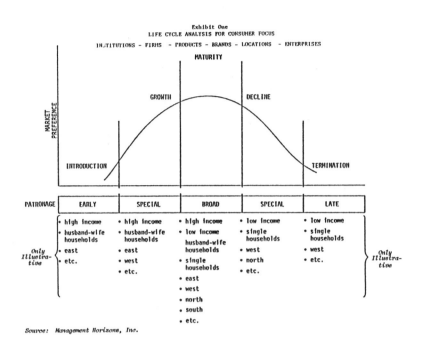

Exhibit One
LIFE CYCLE ANALYSIS FOR CONSUMER FOCUS

INSTITUTIONS - FIRMS - PRODUCTS - BRANDS - LOCATIONS - ENTERPRISES

Source: *Management Horizons, Inc.*

Exhibit Two

Lazarus: Characteristics of Major Competitors for Selected "Problem Departments"		
LAZARUS DEPARTMENT	**MAJOR COMPETITION[1]**	**MAJOR STRATEGIC EMPHASIS OF COMPETITOR**
Toys	Gold Circle (discount department stores)	Well stocked with national brands, lowest price, self-service, heavy seasonal promotion
	Children's Palace (toy and leisure living warehouse-supermarket)	Large stores with wide assortments, warehouse look, classification dominance, self-service
Major Appliances	Sun TV and Appliance (locally dominant specialty chain)	Aggressive promotion of low price image, cluster of convenient locations, carnival atmosphere in stores, personal selling emphasis
	Sears (mall department stores and catalog order stores)	Massive display of only private brands, several models of each product, heavy promotion, with reduced price emphasis, professionally trained salesmen
Female Junior Ready-To-Wear	The Limited and other specialty stores (Casual Corner, Petrie, etc.)	Tight focus on narrow market segment, youth oriented atmosphere, trendy image, sales people available but customers encouraged to browse, limited price range, coordinated merchandise presentations, high traffic mall and downtown locations

[1]Restricted to the two or three major competitors in the Columbus, Ohio market area.

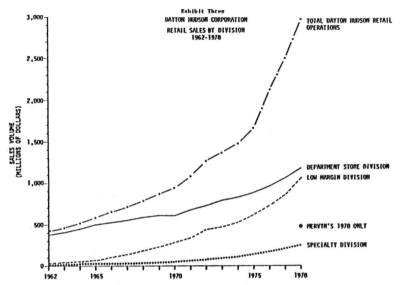

Exhibit Three
DAYTON HUDSON CORPORATION
RETAIL SALES BY DIVISION
1962-1978

Source: Management Horizons analysis of data publicly reported by Dayton Hudson in 10-K reports submitted to the S.E.C.

Exhibit Four GENERAL MILLS BUSINESS UNITS			
Unit	Sales (Millions of $) 1979	% Increase Over 1978	Operating Profit Growth Over 1978
Food Processing	$2062	10.8%	14.3%
Restaurants	436	22.9	18.7
Creative Products	609	23.8	(4.8)
Fashion	360	20.9	(48.6)*
Specialty Retailing The Talbots (10 stores) Eddie Bauer (12) Lee Wards (31) Wallpapers-To-Go (47)	276	17.1	84.7

*Includes a $17.5 million pre-tax loss at Ship & Shore and an $8.5 million after-tax benefit from the termination of the Kimberly Division women's apparel division.

Exhibit Five
Recent Acquisitions and Divestitures

Retailing Entity	Acquired By	Date	Divested To	Date
Ralph's-Northern California	Federated Department Stores	Geographic Expansion	Lucky Stores	1980
Value House Catalog Showrooms	Supermarket General	1971	Service Merchandise	1978
The Union	Manhatten Industries	1969	Marshall Field	1980
Pix Shoes	W. R. Grace	1969	Kobacker Stores	1978
Cartier	Kenton Corp.	1968	Hocq Family	1976
Bonwit Teller	Genesco	1957	Allied Department Stores	1979
Tiffany & Co.	Tiffany & Co. (from Genesco)	1961	Avon Products	1979
Hammacher Schlemmer	Kayser-Roth (acquired by Gulf & Western - 1975)	1960	Bradford Exchange	1980
MacLeod's	Gamble-Skogmo	1947	Can West Capital Corp.	1980
Stedman's	Gamble-Skogmo	1964	Can West Capital Corp.	1980
Joseph Harris	Garfinkel, Brooks Brothers, Miller & Rhoads	1971	Petrie Stores	1979

RETAIL CUSTOMER SATISFACTION AND DISSATISFACTION

Stephen A. Greyser
Harvard Business School/Marketing Science Institute

ABSTRACT

Retailers have a long tradition of concern over customer satisfaction (e.g., "the customer is always right"). However, consumer (and consumerist) dissatisfaction with retailers' performance remains. Retailers need to show both sensitivity to consumer perspectives and responsiveness to distinctive pro-consumer viewpoints. Retailers should demonstrate that they care about the consumer as a person, not just as a "two-legged wallet."

By way of prologue regarding retail customer satisfaction and dissatisfaction, let me make two initial observations. First that consumer satisfaction is a long-term goal of all intelligent retailers. Second, consumerism -- as the institutional manifestation of consumer dissatisfaction -- is still very salient to retail management (as well as to the management of manufacturers who sell through retail channels).

Consumerism was a major force during the 1970's. It can be seen as part of a broader movement by "receiving-enders" in society -- such as welfare parents, prison families, students, and others wishing to have some say in the processes of which they were at the receiving end. Although some observers think that the strength of consumerism has been greatly attenuated, I believe that "consumerism is here to stay," especially in terms of its many accomplishments during the past decade. Much of what consumer activists have pursued has now become institutionalized within business and within government. One need look no further than the complaint-handling procedures among retailers, manufacturers, and even government agencies in 1980 vs. those in 1970 to discern the impact I cite. Nonetheless, many consumers still feel relatively powerless in light of what they perceive as a marketplace imbalance between individual consumers and large institutions (particularly but not exclusively business institutions).

It warrants note that although the aforementioned improvement in complaint-handling ability is correct as to substance and certainly as to procedures, these improvements may well have been matched -- or even outpaced -- by consumer propensities to complain and expectations regarding complaint-handling.

DISTINCTIVE POSITIONING OF RETAILERS

Retailers have a distinctive role in the distribution system, a role that prepares them well for trying to avoid consumer dissatisfaction and being able to address it capably. Retailers are close to consumers on a daily basis (with the possible exception of retail headquarters people). This is in marked contrast to those in manufacturing organizations. Retailers serve as a link between manufacturers and consumers and must listen to and work with both in order to be successful.

Because of this distinctive role, there is a distinctive opportunity for retailers. They can efficiently gather consumer feedback -- on behalf of both themselves and manufacturers. They can serve as a vehicle for resolving complaints, whether the latter be intended for manufacturers or the retail organization itself; the retailer is local and can act relatively more quickly than can the manufacturer in many instances. Retailers have an opportunity to adopt a pro-consumer posture, not only to reduce consumer dissatisfaction but to enhance the pro-consumer image (competitively) of the store.

Retail Traditions

It has been my observation that retailers have been able to adapt to the changes wrought in part by the consumer movement during the past decade more readily than have many in manufacturing companies. Some of this capability may derive from the distinctive positioning just described. Some of it may reflect some enduring retail traditions. "The customer is always right." "Satisfied customers are repeat customers." The former may not always be practiced; the latter may not always manifest itself. Nonetheless, the ethos endures.

... And Perspectives

Yet despite these traditions and the well-intentioned efforts of the vast majority of the retail community, there remains dissatisfaction with the marketplace mechanism and with the retailer's role within it. One major reason for this is that different groups in the marketplace have different views of what goes on in the marketplace. They define the very same marketplace activities in different ways, as my late senior colleague Raymond A. Bauer and I pointed out in the Harvard Business Review article, "The Dialogue That Never Happens."

For example, do high prices simply reflect cost pressures or do they reflect a "consumer be damned" attitude? The latter is often the perception engendered by supermarket overstamping of sequential price increases on old packages. Is advertising principally information or is it an instrument of seduction?

Are store-to-store price variations evidence of competition --
or that "prices could be lower all over?"

These few illustrations -- and there are many more -- reflect the different "mindsets" of those in retail (or most
business) management and those in the activist community.

OPERATING AREAS AFFECTED

The growth of consumerism has impacted on a wide variety
of retail policies, practices, and operating areas. Already
mentioned is that of complaint-handling -- where both the extent of the capability and the procedures for dealing with consumer complaints have improved to the consumer's favor.

Other areas affected include:

● Advertising -- Such terms as "sale," "introductory
  offer," and "list price" now have specific definitions in law in states such as Massachusetts.

● Sales staff training -- Turnover and inadequate
  training cause problems in terms of providing
  information to customers on the sales floor.
  One effort to help overcome some of the problems
  is a creative use by retail floor personnel of
  manufacturer hot-lines; these direct lines to
  trained manufacturer personnel can provide information direct from the source on certain
  kinds of feature-laden goods (e.g., appliances).

● Billing and credit procedures have been very
  much affected by consumerism.

● Consumer information -- The extent of consumer
  information has grown and the nature of that
  information has become more informative on the
  part of both manufacturers and retailers. Most
  of this information is oriented to helping in
  consumer buying decisions, although some has
  been geared more to aiding in consumer buying
  processes, i.e., consumer education materials.

● Product testing and quality -- Particularly for
  major department store and supermarket retailers,
  there have been substantial impacts of consumerism in these areas.

WHAT CONSUMERS THINK

When we examine studies of public attitudes toward retailing and retailer performance, we find that the public looks favorably upon many aspects of retail performance in the marketplace. However, there is an undertone of discontent from some who say "stores don't care about giving consumers a fair deal." Let us look more specifically at some of the data from the Sentry Study of public attitudes toward consumerism, based on the opinions of a national cross-section of over 1500 Americans in the winter of 1977.

The "good news" side of the data is that among some 25 industries, department stores received the second highest rating (32%) for doing a good job for consumers. This good news in terms of relative appraisal is somewhat offset by the absolute level of consumers (44%) who either strongly or somewhat agree with the statement "Most stores don't really care about giving consumers a fair deal." (It should be noted that this percentage is almost the same as that (46%) for a comparable statement about manufacturers.)

The intermediary role that retailers play between manufacturers and consumers is reflected in the very high percentage (77%) of those who say that when they did have a complaint, they complained to a store or dealer; only 21% percent complained directly to a manufacturer.

The unanswerable question regarding these data is whether criticisms at retail only reflect criticisms of manufacturers -- or whether they are truly different.

CONSUMER ORIENTED AND CONSUMERIST ORIENTED

In recent years, many retailers have worked hard to try to be more consumer-oriented and competitive in terms of attracting consumer dollars. This is not, however, the same as being consumerist-oriented. Let me try to illustrate the differences.

To be more consumer-oriented calls for doing a better job of identifying and targeting in on specific market segments. It calls for planning and carrying out better consumer research in order to monitor the needs and wants of those segments. It calls for undertaking better merchandising and promotion to those segments. And it calls for improving knowledge about the products and the store on the part of in-store sales staff.

To be more consumerist-oriented, however, calls for different things. Most of all, it calls for considering customers as having a stake in the relationship between them and the retailer -- and furthermore as being among those whose interests are considered as an input to decisions, rather than simply being "targets." For example, billing and credit procedures should be reviewed from a consumer point of view, rather than simply from the point of view of the store. Advertising should be examined for its clarity and straightforwardness of information, not simply its persuasive ability. Where feasible, stores should conduct their own product testing. Information/ education programs should be considered to help consumers be more intelligent buyers in various product categories.

Overall, being consumerist-oriented calls for fostering an attitude of concern with the consumer as a person, not just a "two-legged wallet."

Coordinated Consumer Policy for Retailers

Retailers should have a coordinated consumer policy. In my opinion, this requires a formal consumer affairs entity within the organizational structure of the retailing firm. This entity would have three principal audiences -- the internal audience of management, the activist and consumer representative community, and consumers themselves. This approach of a formal organizational unit provides a stronger basis for consumerist-oriented input in retailer decision-making than does the approach of asking various organizational units to "consider the consumerist perspective" in their decision-making. The single entity basically has a mix of roles: on the one hand, it is the company's representative to the consumer, on the other it is the consumer's representative to the company. In short, it has a "bridge" role within dual expertises in retail operations and consumer affairs.

Such a unit should have support from and access to top management in the retailing firm. It should conduct programs to sensitize staff members to the kinds of consumer concerns described above. It should establish vehicles for two-way flow with consumer organizations and with consumers themselves. (The Stop & Shop Companies' long-time "consumer boards" are a good illustration.) The unit's responsibilities would include serving as a consumer-oriented "screen" for reviewing the policies and practices of the retail firm, as well as serving as an internal information source regarding consumer attitudes, legislative and regulatory trends, etc.

This kind of unit would help to incorporate consumer satisfaction as one of the measures of retailer effectiveness. Obviously, such traditional and important factors as sales, margin percentages, and profits will remain. My point is that the degree of customer/consumer satisfaction is an additional and useful measure of effectiveness in retailing.

Sensitivity and Responsiveness

Through such an approach retailers can do a better job of showing both sensitivity and responsiveness to the broadened and heightened consumer concerns of today. In the course of doing this, retailers may find merchandising opportunities that represent a competitive advantage. In the early days of consumerism, a number of supermarket firms found just such a merchandising opportunity in developing unit pricing for their own stores in advance of legal requirements; the existence of unit pricing (and the opportunity to advertise it as a differentiated feature) served several major chains well.

One further aspect of trying to demonstrate sensitivity and responsiveness is to have an understanding of consumer expectations and how to match them. And -- like the effective merchandisers that good retailers are -- in trying to be just a little bit ahead in these areas will often come perceived superiority. Retailers have long recognized that consumers do have ultimate power in the marketplace. Today, the thinking retailer (in my opinion) recognizes that consumer power extends beyond simply their buying capability.

SUMMARY

Let me offer a brief summary of my principal points.

First, consumerism is still alive and meaningful for the business community generally and for retailers specifically. Second, retailers have a distinctive role and opportunity because of their position as "middlemen" in the distribution system. Further, retailing has some significant pro-consumer-traditions.

Fourth, different groups (and different people) have different perspectives on the very same activities in the marketplace; what the retailer may see as very traditional marketplace behavior on the firm's part may be viewed with suspicion by the skeptical consumer of today.

Fifth, the advent and growth of consumerism affect a wide variety of retail policies, practices, and operating areas. On the whole, however, the public looks favorably upon retailers' performance in the marketplace, although almost half the public agrees that "stores don't care about giving consumers a fair deal."

Sixth, there is an important difference between being consumer-oriented and consumerist-oriented. The latter, in my opinion, calls for a coordinated consumer policy through a single consumer affairs entity with support from and access to top management; this unit should serve in a "bridge" role as the company's representative to consumers, as well as the consumer's representative to the firm.

Finally, in today's consumer environment, retailers need to show both sensitivity to consumer concerns and responsiveness to consumer perspectives. Retailers should demonstrate that they care about the consumer as a person -- not just as a "two-legged wallet."

REFERENCES

Bauer, Raymond A. and Stephen A. Greyser (1967), "The Dialogue That Never Happens," Harvard Business Review, (November-December).

McNair, Malcolm P. and Eleanor G. May (1976), The Evolution of Retail Institutions in the United States, Marketing Science Institute Monograph.

St. Marie, Satenig (1977), "The Future of Consumerism in Retailing," Journal of Retailing (Fall).

Sentry Study of "Consumerism at the Crossroads" (1977), Sentry Insurance Company.

RETAILING AND THE PRODUCTION OF POPULAR CULTURE

Elizabeth C. Hirschman
New York University

ABSTRACT

Material culture consists of the symbolic artifacts
(i.e. products) of a society. The primary thesis of the
present paper is that retailing serves as a central institution in the production of cultural symbols. Discussion
focuses upon two aspects of retailer influence on symbol
production: (1) the internal creation of symbols by retailers, and (2) retailer influence upon external producers
of symbols.

INTRODUCTION

Material culture consists of those symbolic artifacts
produced by a society; it represents the tangible products of
a society (Smelser 1972). Researchers in marketing and consumer behavior have frequently examined the process of production for individual symbols of material culture (e.g. a new
type of toothpaste, automobile or apparel); but they have
rarely focused attention upon the aggregate effects of this
process. Because a macro perspective has been applied infre-
quently to the analysis of material culture, we have perhaps
neglected some of the more significant aspects of its impact
on marketing and consumer behavior.

Although isolated efforts have been made to call attention
to the value which a 'sociology of consumption' perspective may
have for research (e.g. Nicosia and Mayer 1976, Zaltman and
Wallendorf 1977), few theoretical or empirical responses have
followed. The present paper uses such a perspective to examine
the role of retailing as an institution having central importance to the production of material culture.

The primary thesis is that retailing serves as a central
institution in the production of cultural symbols. For purpose
of this discussion, the institution of retailing will be defined as constituting those agencies and their related processes which conduct direct exchanges with private consumers.[1]
With the exception of symbols that are self-produced or con-

---

[1]Thus, industrial and government exchanges are excluded.

sumed in the production of other symbols, retailing has primary responsibility for processes that make cultural symbols available to consumers.

Cultural symbols may be dichotomized, somewhat arbitrarily, into two categories: (1) high culture and (2) popular culture (Lowenthal 1961, MacDonald 1961). The term high culture refers to symbols that are dominantly aesthetic and subjective in their attribute structure and, as Levy (1978) describes them, "fall on a continuum of social value or prestige at a level regarded as particularly meritorious or qualified. They include symphonic music, ballet, modern dance, opera, painting, sculpture, legitimate theatre, etc." Conversely, products implied by the term popular culture are those aspects of material culture that Peterson (1979, p. 139) has normatively characterized as "crassly commercial ... avowedly devoted to making a profit by 'giving people what they want.'" Popular culture symbols . include such products as apparel, automobiles, movies and cosmetics.

Because a considerable amount of research is already underway on retail processes regarding high culture (e.g. Holbrook 1980, Levy and Czepiel 1974, Becker 1978), this paper concentrates on popular culture. This area has been dealt with to a limited extent from a sociological perspective (e.g. Hirschman and Stampfl 1980, Schenk and Holman 1980), but not using an institutional framework for analysis, as is the case here. The paper discusses the creation of popular culture and its relationship to retailing. A general discussion of current sociological theory precedes a focused discussion of retail-related influences. Propositions are presented within each general and focused discussion to organize the material presented.

THE PRODUCTION OF POPULAR CULTURE

The assertion that popular culture is produced originates with the observation "that symbolic elements of culture do not spring forth full-blown, but rather are made somewhere by someone" (Peterson 1979, p. 152). The majority of present popular culture symbols were introduced into society by specialists whose task it is to create and communicate such symbols (Peterson 1979). As societies increase in complexity, there is a growing separation between these symbol specialists and those who consumes the symbols (Blau 1975). Further, there results an increasingly systematized and specialized process of symbol production and communication. The production of culture perspective rests on the assumption that the organizational form of these specialized activities, for example the institution of retailing, will substantially influence the development, content and meaning of the symbols produced.

Retailing and the Production of Popular Culture

The role of retailing in the production of popular culture is a complex one, but centers around two related processes: (1) the internal production of symbols by retailers and (2) retailer influence over external producers of symbols. Retailers exercise direct control over the production of many symbols of popular culture, because they are directly responsible for their manufacture.

The dominant retailers of general merchandise in the United States, i.e. Sears, K Mart, J. C. Penney, Woolworth, Federated and Wards, generate combined annual sales in excess of $57 billion per year. These sales represent consumer expenditures for product symbols of popular culture which are, in large part, produced directly or under the strict guidance of the retail organizations distributing them. Thus, Sears and other vertically integrated retail systems that conduct the majority of retail transactions (Mason and Mayer 1978), are in many instances the producers of popular culture and not merely its distributors.

The decisions made by retailers regarding the products they will manufacture influence the production of many popular culture symbols. Although one vertically integrated retail organization, by itself, has less than a significant impact on the production of popular culture, all such retailers considered together may have a major influence on the production of these symbols.

Further, retailer influence over the production of popular culture extends beyond direct manufacture. Retailing organizations which display horizontal, as opposed to vertical, integration such as Federated Department Stores or the Dayton-Hudson Corporation, also possess substantial ability to influence the decisions of external agencies that manufacture products for them. The purchasing power of such retail organizations, especially when it is combined under the auspices of a central buying cooperative such as the Associated Merchandise Corporation, can exert large influence over sources of supply. External vendors may adjust their production schedules and content to fulfill the demands of major retail organizations. Thus, whether by direct manufacture or by indirect influence over the processes of production, retailing as an institution may influence the form and content of popular culture.

Implications of Retailing Control of Symbol Production

There are several implications to arise from the notion that retailing influences the production of popular culture. Among the more obvious normative implications is the proposition that popular culture reflects not so much the desires and values of the consuming public, as it does the desires and values of decision makers within the retail system.

There is no inherent guarantee that the combined desires of retail decision makers concerning what symbols will be produced are congruent with those of the consuming public. The argument that 'retailers who do not cater to the desires of the consumer soon go out of business' may be valid on a micro-organizational basis; but is specious when applied to retailing as a collectivity. The consumer must choose from among that set of products made available (Hirschman and Stampfl 1980). He/she may attempt to optimize satisfaction within the set of available products by switching patronage from one retailer to another. Yet, consumers individually or in aggregate have little real power to influence the set of symbols with which they are presented.

This is because consumer demand is most often measured by retailers in a _post_ _hoc_ fashion using historic sales levels for products already in the merchandise mix (i.e. symbol set) of the retailer. In contrast, the elements of the merchandise mix, itself, are generally selected on an _a_ _priori_ basis using input from industry and trade sources, retail purchasing agent subjective criteria and other non-consumer-generated sources of information (Hirsch 1972, Blumer 1969, Barnett 1959). Thus, retail sales levels of particular products represent a measure of relative consumer acceptance of presently available symbols, rather than consumer desire for actual and potential symbols (Hirschman and Stampfl 1980).

A central issue in this regard is the extent to which symbol-producing retail organizations "manage and control values and knowledge rather than simply purvey" (Lane 1970, p. 240). The position put forward here is that the increasing tendency of retailing toward vertical integration has a profound impact on the ability of this institution to control consumer values and symbol meaning. Vertical organization of retailing may substantially affect not only patterns of retail competitive structure but also the types of products retailing chooses to create.

One important proposition in this regard is that vertical integration works to make the symbol set created by retailers more homogeneous. Several advantages accrue to retailers as a result of homogenization. Greater homogenization of the symbol set within one retail organization enhances distribution efficiency and simplifies decision making (Mason and Mayer 1978). Presumably the more similar the content and meaning of the products carried, the more similar are the organizational requirements for producing, distributing and communicating them. Further, product homogeneity enables retailers to accumulate more

74

specialized expertise regarding marketing processes and to more accurately forecast both supply and demand levels.

As individual retail organizations work to homogenize their product assortments, an increasing homogeneity of popular culture may occur. That this is so is evidenced by the fact that an increasingly smaller set of retail organizations is responsible for the production of an increasingly larger proportion of symbols (Mason and Mayer 1978). The symbols created by these organizations are more homogeneous than those offered by their predecessors, due to system requirements for standardization and internal consistency. In contrast, earlier, nonintegrated retailers operated predominately on a free-form basis marked by greater heterogeneity both in organizational framework and symbols produced. Hence, the proposition is made that the overall variability of the popular culture symbol set available to consumers is reduced due to the increased presence of vertical integration within retail organizations.[2]

This proposition is supported by sociological studies. Peterson and Berger (1975) for example, note the influence of market structure upon the production process in the music industry. Surveying industry and aesthetic data from 1948 to 1973, they show that in periods of atomistic competition, musical styles are diverse, while in periods of ologopoly, music is much more homogeneous. More recently Chapple and Garofalo (1977) have reached similar conclusions.

MACRO INFLUENCE OF RETAILING ON SOURCES OF SUPPLY

The general propositions just presented may be applied on a more abstract level to three sources of symbols distributed by

---

[2]Note that this proposition is stated on a macro basis across all consumers. On a micro-level, quite a different result should occur. As a result of increasing vertical integration, an individual consumer is likely to be exposed to a more heterogeneous symbol set than in the past because of the greater number of retail outlets which carry products to which the consumer may be exposed. A vertically integrated retail system may carry the same products from coast to coast (macro homogeneity); yet on a local level the consumer is exposed to more retail outlets than in the past, resulting in greater micro heterogeneity. Moore (1974 p. 114) comments on this phenomenon "The very mass production that yields uniformity ... also yields the possibility of substantial variability in the combinations that particular consuming units may choose to put together."

retailing: the Arts, Crafts and Ethnic Groups. Each of these three areas serves as a symbol resource for retailing; many, perhaps the majority, of retail symbols originate within the domains of arts, crafts or ethnic groups. The ways in which these symbols are chosen for retail mass distribution, together with the impact retail activities may have on the originating systems, are described below.

High Culture as a Source of Retail Symbols

Through processes of transformation, symbols originally produced within high culture (i.e. the arts) may be later reproduced as popular culture for distribution by retailing. Symbols originating within high culture may be reintroduced as symbols of popular culture by either direct or selective routes. In cases of direct derivation, symbols created by high culture milieux are commercialized by retailing in a way that keeps intact their superficial characteristics.

Examples of direct derivation would include prints of famous paintings, reproductions of sculpture or historic artifacts, copies of architectural styles, and performances of plays from the legitimate theater at a dinner theater or as movies. In these instances most of the overt features of the original art form remain intact; they are simply transcribed into a context that is produced and distributed on a mass basis and at a price level commensurate with a larger scale of consumer demand.

In other cases certain aspects of high culture art forms may be incorporated into popular culture symbols to enhance their retail marketability. This represents a selective derivation approach to the creation of popular culture. For example, rock musicians creating popular culture symbols may construct a series of songs around an operatic framework adapted from high culture.[3] The choice of which aspects of high culture will be used in such a selective way is based primarily upon estimations of their commercial viability.

The dominant criterion for both direct and selective derivation from high culture to popular culture is that of profitability (Becker 1978). High culture symbols that meet stringent aesthetic criteria may never the less be rejected for popularization, because it is believed they would not be profitable on a mass consumption basis. The critical issue is the anticipated generalizability of the content of the symbol; this is based upon retailer expectations that the symbol will strike a responsive chord among a large enough segment of the market to assure commercial viability. Hence, one is more likely to find

---

[3]For example, rock composer Peter Townshend (the Who) has written two "rock operas" - Tommy and Quadrophenia.

"universally appealing" plays such as "The Sound of Music" reproduced as movies than Arthur Miller's "The Price" or Tom Stop-
pard's "Rosencrantz and Guildenstern Are Dead."

Crafts as a Source of Retail Symbols

A second source of retail symbols is crafts; crafts are
organized systems for producing objects primarily designed to
fulfill utilitarian functions (Becker 1978). Typical craft-ori-
ginating symbols would include furniture, eating utensils, pot-
tery, baskets, fabric, tanned leather, and apparel. Craft-ori-
ginating symbols, like art symbols, may have aesthetic qualities.
However, the critical distinction between the two is their primary function. A craft symbol is created _primarily_ to fulfill a
utilitarian function, for example, to hold water or to protect
the body. An art symbol, conversely, is created _primarily_ to
fulfill an _aesthetic_ function; it is appreciated in and of itself (e.g. its beauty, its poignance) and not for its usefulness
in fulfilling some utilitarian requirement.

Because of their origination as objects having broad utilitarian demand in society, craft symbols are inherently a part of
popular culture. However, their role as symbols of popular culture extends beyond their utilitarian function; they frequently
serve aesthetic purposes as well. In most societies craft objects are inscribed with aesthetic features, such as decorative
coloring, in addition to their required utilitarian features.
These supplemental aesthetic qualities serve to provide an additional basis upon which the craft object can be evaluated and
given meaning. Aesthetic features enlarge the symbolic _capacity_
of the craft object by transforming it from a homogeneous, generic entity to one that may be made individualized and distinctive.

Once the craft object possesses some features that are
unique to it and that serve to differentiate it from function-
ally similar objects (e.g. a red vs. blue pair of shoes), it can
play a much larger role as a cultural symbol. Based upon these
aesthetic features, consumers can form additional subjective as-
sociations with the craft object and endow it with meaning
greatly exceeding its utilitarian purpose (e.g. Hirschman 1980).

In less technologically advanced social systems, craft objects are typically constructed by skilled specialists (i.e.
craftsmen) on a 'by-hand' basis. The production processes underlying such handicrafts differ from those typifying the production of crafts in technologically-advanced societies in two important ways. First, there is inherently greater variability in
craft symbols produced by hand than there is in those produced
by machine. Each handmade item is, to a greater or lesser extent, distinct from its counterparts. In contrast, craft objects produced by machine display much more uniformity in con-

struction. In fact, one of the primary criteria for the "assembly-line" production of crafts is quality control. Interitem variance is purposely minimized and deviants are eliminated or sold as "seconds."

A second important difference between crafts produced in a handicraft mode versus those produced by machine is the nature of the exchange between maker and purchaser. The craftman who constructs an object for sale usually has direct contact with the purchaser. The closeness of this interaction permits a much greater potential for the incorporation of the purchaser's expressed desires into the craft object before, or as, it is being made. In contrast, when craft objects are created on a mass produced, machine-made basis, there is little or no opportunity for the unique wishes of the individual to be incorporated into the product.[4] The utilitarian and aesthetic decisions made regarding the craft symbol are controlled by the producer, not the purchaser.

Ethnic Groups as Sources of Retail Symbols

A third source of popular culture symbols is ethnic groups. Ethnic groups are defined by Glaser and Moynihan (1975, p. 4) as "groups of a society characterized by a distinct sense of difference owing to culture and descent ..." Ethnic groups frequently develop unique sets of symbols that are adopted by group members to aid in intra-group identification and promote inter-group differentiation. Such symbols help members identify one another and set themselves apart from the larger social system (Barth 1969). Examples of ethnic group symbols would include "Afro" hair styles and dashikis (Blacks), bagels and yarmulkes (Jews), and crucifixes (Catholics).

As the popularity of, or identification with, an ethnic group grows within the surrounding social system, the symbols that had served to uniquely identify members of the group may be adopted by nonmembers and become diffused more widely through out society. This diffusion process in enhanced by the activities of retailers who co-opt ethnic symbols they estimate may be popularized (Peterson 1979). For example, the Afro hair style used by militant Blacks in the late 1960's has now become widely diffused outside the boundaries of this ethnic group, largely through the efforts of retailers. Once an ethnic group symbol has become broadly diffused as a cultural symbol, it may be discarded by the originating group, because it no longer serves as a way of establishing and promoting the ethnic bound-

[4] An example of "little" opportunity for purchaser input is the purchase of an automobile having some "custom" features. An example of "no" opportunity is the purchase of a pair of gloves from a department store.

ary (e.g. Peterson 1979, Barth 1969).

RETAILING INFLUENCES UPON ARTS, CRAFTS AND ETHNIC GROUPS

Since retailing acquires symbols from these three sources, it also may substantially impact them as production systems (Crane 1976). The combined decisions by retailers as a collectivity to produce and distribute certain art, craft or ethnic symbols can have profound effects. First, there is the influence that financial resources flowing from retailing to the origins of these symbols may have on the evaluative criteria used by the symbol creators. Second, financial resources flowing from retailing to the origins of these symbols may alter the content of future symbols produced by these sources.

This is because financial flows often serve as an important reward/reinforcement mechanism. Artisans whose products are favored by retailers (i.e. are selected for mass distribution) are provided with the financial resources with which to expand and increase their output. This can result not only in an increase in the proportionate representation of these "favored" artisans' products in the total output of that source of supply, but may also significantly affect the criteria used by "less-favored" artisans. These individuals typically will modify their own products to make them more congruent with those of the "favored" supplier/artisan (Crane 1976).

Numerous examples of this phenomenon may be cited: the many rock-and-roll "clones" that imitated the Beatles during the Sixties; the numerous science fiction movies that followed the successful run of Star Wars; the fashion designers whose clothes closely approximate those of Yves Saint Laurent (haute couture) and Calvin Klein (pret a porter). The shifting of Broadway comedy to follow the lead of Neil Simon and of television comedy to follow that of Norman Lear are relevant examples in the realm of entertainment.

In each of these cases, the retail success of one artisan resulted not only in the increased distribution of and consumer exposure to that artisan's products, but also in the shifting of creative criteria to favor the successful prototype. Thus retail success for a symbol and its creator (as measured in financial flows) may serve not only to increase the production of that creator's symbols, but also to shift the evaluative criteria within the art or craft production system as a whole.

A second impact which retail mass distribution may have upon both arts and crafts is a general flattening of symbol meaning. As was noted earlier, when symbols are selected for retail distribution as popular culture symbols, it is because they are believed to possess a universal appeal (or at least appeal to a market segment large enough to guarantee their profitability). To emphasize this universal appeal, symbols may be shorn of their distinctive and potentially distractive or disturbing elements before they are mass produced. Uncommon fabrics, language, values and so forth are systematically deleted or minimized.

Thus consumers whose only experience with a haute couture fashion is a "knock-off" (i.e. imitation) from Sears or with the legitimate theater is the movie rendition of "California Suite" are consuming symbols that may lack much of the detailed richness and diversity they possessed in their original forms. One normative issue to be considered is whether consumers suffer more "damage" from being exposed to a diluted representation of the original symbol than they would from complete nonexposure to the symbol. Salient to this issue, of course, is how far from the original symbol the mass produced version has strayed.

The foregoing discussion has emphasized primarily the impacts of retail institutional processes upon symbols originating in arts and crafts. A third source of popular culture symbols to be addressed is that of ethnic groups. As noted earlier, when ethnic groups increase in popularity, the demand for their symbols may increase among consumers, generally. The widespread diffusion of the Afro hairstyle is an example of this process.[5] Retailers are, of course, eager to assist this diffusion process because it represents a viable demand segment that they can profitably fulfill.

There is, however, a series of important consequences, both positive and negative, set in motion as a result of widespread retail dissemination of ethnic symbols. First, a positive result is that consumers outside the ethnic group are able to enhance their self-image by adopting the symbols of an ethnic group with which they wish to identify. A consumer who wishes to express an appreciation for American Indian culture may now do so by purchasing these artifacts in a local department store. However, a second, less positive result is that the diffusion of ethnic group symbols outside the boundaries of the group may serve to dilute ethnic identity. Group boundaries are weakened by the external dissemination of internal symbols.

The net result of this process is that ethnic diversity within a society is reduced. It is an interesting paradox that

---

[5]Ethnic group symbols may also diffuse because they are simply judged to have advantages relative to competitive products; for example the increasing diffusion of the bagel (a Jewish ethnic bread) may be cited in this regard.

as ethnic symbols become widespread, largely through the efforts
of retail mass distribution, their potency as ethnic discrimina-
tors diminishes. Thus Peterson (1979) makes the cogent observation that retail processes tend to bind ethnic groups more
firmly into society; the ability of ethnic groups to differentiate themselves from the surrounding population is substantially weakened by the dissemination of their symbols as elements
of popular culture. As Peterson notes (1979 p. 148) "What begins in revolt, ends in style."

SUMMARY

The overall impact of retail institutional processes is
posited to result in a reduction of variance within the three
sources of supply discussed: the arts, crafts, and ethnic
groups. The result of this is an increase in the homogeneity
of the popular culture symbol set made available to society as
a whole. The factors contributing to this effect on a societal
basis are the financial flows emanating from retailers to symbol originators. These financial flows serve as a mechanism
for selective reinforcement of 'favored' artisans; such a differential reward structure works to increase the output of certain artisans and cause competitive artisans to imitate the
symbols produced by those most successful.

On an institutional basis, the dual trends toward vertical
integration and symbol set homogenization among retailers are
self-reinforcing. One contributes to and enhances the other.
This does not mean that the individual consumer is confronted
with a less diverse set of symbols, but rather that the overall
set of symbols produced by a society is more homogeneous. It
is believed that the intensity of institutional influences
generated by retailing will increase in the future, as pressures
for profitability, efficiency and organizational control increase. Institutional systematization increases the need for
and ability to insure standardization of products. Hence, as
the institution of retailing becomes increasingly systematic,
greater homogenization of outputs should result.

REFERENCES

Barrett, James H., "The Sociology of Art." In Sociology Today,
    edited by Robert K. Meston, Leonard Boom, and Leonard S.
    Coltrell, Jr. New York: Basic Books, 1959.

Barth, Fredrick, Ethnic Groups and Boundaries, Boston: Little,
    Brown and Company, 1969.

81

Becker, Howard S., "Arts and Crafts", American Journal of Sociology, Vol. 83, January 1978, 862-889.

Blau, Peter, Approaches to the Study of Social Structure, New York: The Free Press, 1975.

Bluner, Herbert, "Fashion: From Class Differentiation to a Collective Selection", Sociological Quarterly, 10 (ummer) 1969: 275-91.

Chapple, S. and Garofalo, R., Rock N Roll is Here to Pay: The History and Politics of the Music Industry. Chicago: Nelso Hall, 1977.

Crane, Diane, "Reward Systems in Art, Science and Religion", In The Production of Culture, ed. R. A. Peterson, Beverly Hills, Co.: Sage, 1976, 57-72.

Glazer, Nathan and Daniel P. Moynihan, Ethnicity, Cambridge: Harvard University Press, 1975.

Hirsch, Paul M., "Processing Fads and Fashions: An Organization Set Analysis of Cultural Industry Systems." American Journal of Sociology, 1972, 639-59.

Hirschman, Elizabeth C., "Attributes of Attributes and Layers of Meaning" in Advances in Consumer Research, Vol. 7, Association for Consumer Research, forthcoming 1980.

_____, and Ronald W. Stampfl, "The Roles of Retailing in the Diffusion of Popular Culture: Four Micro Perspectives", Journal of Retailing, Spring 1980.

Holbrook, Morris, "Consumer Esthetics: Emerging Theory, Methods and Marketing Applications," Forthcoming, Advances in Consumer Research, Vol. 7, Association for Consumer Research, 1980.

Lane, Micheal, "Books and Their Publishers." In Media Sociology, edited by Jeremy Tunstall. Urbana: University of Illinois Press, 1970.

Levy, Sidney J., "Aesthetic Attributes and Arts Consumers," paper presented to the Marketing the Arts: Issues, Perspectives and Pragmatics Confernece, September 28-30, 1978, Spring Hill Center, Wayzata, Minnesota.

_____, and John A. Czepiel, "Marketing and Aesthitics", Proceedings, American Marketing Association, 1974, 386-391.

Lowenthal, Leo, Literature, Popular Culture and Society (N.Y.: Prentice-Hall, 1961).

MacDonald, Dwight, Masscult and Midcult (N.Y.: Partisan Review 1961).

Mason, J. Barry and Morris Mayer, Modern Retailing: Theory and Practice, Dallas: Business Publications, Inc., 1978.

Nicosia, Francesco and Mayer, Robert N., "Toward A Sociology of Consumption," Journal of Consumer Research, Vol. 3, 1976, 65-25.

Peterson, Richard A., "Revitalizing the Culture Concept", in Annual Review of Sociology, Vol. 5, 1979, 137-66.

_____, and David G. Berger, "Cycles in Symbol Production: The Case of Popular Music", American Sociological Review, 1975, 158-73.

Schenk, Carolynn and Rebecca H. Holman, "A Sociological Approach to Brand Choice: The Situational Self Image," in Advances in Consumer Research, Association for Consumer Research, 1980

Smelser, Neil J., Sociology, Second Edition, New York: John Wiley and Sons, 1972.

Zaltman, Gerald and Wallendorf, Melanie, "Sociology: The Missing Chunk or How We've Missed the Boat," in Contemporary Marketing Thought, eds. Barnett A. Greenberh and Danny N. Bellenger, Chicago: American Marketing Association, 1977.

RETAILING THEORY:
SOME CRITICISM AND SOME ADMIRATION

Stanley C. Hollander
Michigan State University, East Lansing

ABSTRACT

Retailing has been the subject of extensive explicit (and constant implicit) theorizing. Macrotheory has concentrated on environmental relationships and on institutional evolution. The greatest needs are for more rigorous institutional taxonomies, greater knowledge of customer shopping satisfactions, and more precise externality measures.

Introduction

Self-conscious, explicit theorizing may be harmful to a merchant's career. In a gossipy, somewhat malicious and therefore interesting book Harris (1979) claims that E. A. Filene was removed from Filene store management because his strongly articulated theories (e.g., model stock plan, automatic markdown basement, employee democracy) ranged from brilliant to potentially destructive. Similarly, Richard Weil, Jr., a member of the owning family, ceased to be president of Macy's New York shortly after a New Yorker profile (Macdonald 1952) called him the one true abstract thinker in the trade.

Nevertheless, retailers use many implicit theories. They start from one basic premise—that the world contains many continuing regularities—and derive numerous working hypotheses. They believe that people who slink around the store in warm weather wearing loose, bulky coats with many inner pockets are up to no good; that gift sales will peak before Christmas, and that impulse goods should be displayed in high traffic locations.

Academicians' choices of retail research topics, such as location, image, shelf exposure, and price effects also indicate implicit beliefs or theories about both relevance and probable regularities as well as, perhaps, estimates of topic manageability and acceptability for publication. The range of such research will astonish anyone who has not worked through the bibliographies and finding guides (Hollander 1978b).

Yet much more theorizing is needed. For example, conventional department store merchants have been steadily dividing their apparel departments into ever-growing numbers of "lifestyle" sections. This process should have been based on some well-tested theories about: (a) the way operating costs and inventory investments vary with the size of the merchandising units and (b) the way customers shop and identify departments. But few merchants will admit to knowing how many customers cross-shop what combinations of life-style departments and whether those customers find the segmentation either helpful or even meaningful.

Now Kurt Salmon Associates (1979) reports that excessive subdivision is confusing to the customers and costly to the stores. T. Dart Ellsworth made the same point in 1977. These criticisms may be right or wrong, but unfortunately we have few proven principles that help distinguish between functional and dysfunctional segmentation.

Meanwhile we have some raw material for theories about follow-the-leader behavior among retailers. We should, however, also recognize the way customer expectations demand conformity among stores.

The great bulk of explicit theorizing about, for, and in the retail trades may be divided between: (a) macrotheory, concerned primarily with the general behavior of retail institutions, the way they impose and receive costs and benefits on and from society, and their other relationships with the larger environment, and (b) microtheory which deals with managerial strategy and tactics. This paper will concentrate on macrotheory.

Macrotheories often seem Olympian and devoid of managerial relevance. But by defining hospitable and hostile conditions for various types of trade they delineate opportunities, validate performance measurements and underlie the more applied middle range theories. The term "theory" here implies broadly based statements that explain or predict repetitive retail behavior or that help describe retailing in new or more meaningful ways. This loose definition will not attempt to distinguish between principles, laws, theories, hypotheses and propositions on the basis of breadth, depth, power or degree of proof. Since theory involves generalization it is usually situationally incomplete and can only support, not supplant, judgment, skill, intuition and experience.

We should distinguish between general marketing theory, which deals with a broad range of exchanges in balancing heterogeneous demands and supplies, and retailing theory per se, which relates to the specific roles, characteristics and operations of retailers and retail institutions in effectuating those exchanges.

Emphasis will be placed on the deficiencies of the theories cited below, i.e., on the work that remains to be done since the purpose of this conference is to move ahead rather than bask in mutual adulation. That should not obscure admiration for the substantive and heuristic contributions of our theoretical predecessors.

Economic Development

Economic anthropologists disagree (Hollander 1978a) but many feel that retailing plays its biggest social role at relatively moderate states of economic development. Retailers are relatively worldly, marginal people in peasant cultures, and often provide business, legal, matrimonial, personal and medical advice (Fallers 1962). They have occupied this role in the settlement of the American West and the current Hispanic barrios of Chicago (Kizilbash and Carmen 1975-76). When endowed with locational monopolies, retailers in such cultures will help their clients advance economically until their progress might threaten the monopoly, at which point the merchants will try to stifle growth (Adams 1963). In the poorer nations retailing is often both a training ground and a source of capital for potential industrialists, but in more prosperous countries industry generates its own recruits (Alexander 1968). Retailing methods in the poorer societies often seem cumbersome, inefficient, wasteful of both perishable products and human labor and unlikely to stimulate supply improvements. But in the existing context and in the absence of effective channel redesign they may be the lowest unit cost distribution methods available (Holton 1953). Both attitudinal and financial problems usually make consumer cooperation much less viable than commercial retailing in the less developed countries.

Much theorizing about retailing and economic development rests upon a short-lived wave of government-financed overseas marketing teaching and research between the mid-1950's and mid-1970's. More work might have provided more answers and some interesting projects continue.

Macromodels

At a more general level the Marketing Science Institute's CRIM (Customer-Retailer Interaction Model) was a very broad theory intended for American and other environments (Halbert 1965). It showed both final customer and retailer inventories which fluctuated in response to actual flows and perceptions of present and future demand-supply conditions. Inventory was defined to include goods, services, skills and techniques.

Financial considerations and operating costs (including shopping pleasure as a negative cost) occupied peripheral positions. The scheme glossed over such questions as why should a retailer seek to satisfy one set of demands rather than another; what are the mediating factors through which supply and demand perceptions filter; and what is the role of competition. The model is not used at present.

Baranoff (1965), who was involved with CRIM, presented another and more appealing model. Here group behavior (perceptions, goals, power, knowledge, organization and flexibility) and retailing employ instruments and resources drawn from, and influencing, the environment to supply goods and services to match customer needs and wants and provide a bundle of considerations labeled "convenience." Baranoff explicitly rejected any specific place for competition in order to make the model culture-free. A totally culture-free model might have recognized non-commercial goals, such as purposefully inconvenient government liquor stores designed to reduce consumption. In such comprehensive models, I think, attempts at parsimony, the desire to lump many different things in one square or circle, hide the basic questions and relationships.

Customer Satisfactions

Fuller models will provide much more detail on customer relations. The Journal of American Culture (Fishwick 1978) humanistically probed the social, cultural, religious, aesthetic, psychological and symbolic roles of one retail firm, McDonald's Restaurants, in American life. If its authors are correct, eating a double cheeseburger is no insignificant event. Hirschman and Stampfl (1980) also present an insightful discussion of retailing's cultural influence.

Tauber (1972) provided a useful intuitive catalog of the social, sensory and kinesthetic satisfactions that shopping might provide. Sadly, little has been done to measure the importance of those satisfactions or the ways they might be induced. Likert-scale questions may not elicit valid responses, so observation and experimentation are needed as well. McDonald's supposedly believes that children feel useful and happy when fetching napkins if the dispensers are kept on the counters rather than the tables, but one wonders how that belief has been tested. (Perhaps such tests might show that people use more coatsleeves and fewer napkins when the dispensers are kept away from the tables.) Validated concepts of in-store shopping satisfactions would be very helpful in predicting the acceptability of in-home systems.

One approach to determining what stores mean to customers has been through shopper typologies based upon Stone's (1954) seminal economic, personalizing, ethical and apathetic shopper categories. Subsequent writers have in part reaffirmed Stone's groupings and in part added new types, such as price, entertainment and prestige shoppers. The concept remains appealing, but the way individuals shift from one category to another with variations in item and/or purchase situations should be studied. Alderson (1957) did talk about instrumental, congenial and symptomatic shopping rather than shoppers, but most typologies implicitly assume that an individual will act uniformly in all shopping events. The other great need is for behavioral rather than purely attitudinal data. Williams, Painter and Nichols (1978) have at least correlated stated choice of favorite store with a grocery shopper taxonomy.

Institutional Evolution

Another major theorizing approach tries to describe, and sometimes explain and/or predict, institutional evolution. Dreesmann (1968) created a rich biological analogy. The labels match, e.g., new types are called mutations, but aside from a "survival of the fittest" Darwinism, the applicability of other biological laws, such as those of genetic inheritance, remain unproven.

Other major, more specific, patterns described here last year (Hollander 1980) include McNair's (1958) Wheel of Retailing (new types start low in price, markup, operating cost and prestige, gradually climb and become vulnerable), Davidson et al.'s (1976) Life Cycle· (new types grow, mature and decline), Hower's (1943) Accordian (alternating market domination by stores with wide and narrow assortments), and Gist's (1968) Retail Hegelianism (synthesis will emerge after a retail type is attacked by its antithesis).

These models can be compared with Hirschman's (1978) Theory of Natural Market Dominance in GAF merchandise retailing. She holds that three types of department stores--conventional ones, national chain branches and discount units--have and do use one stop shopping advantages, or "concentrated variety," to dominate upper, middle and lower level consumer markets. Each also has advantages in selling certain goods.

But these three institutional types have not always occupied their current positions. Accordian-like, conventional department stores have narrowed merchandise assortments from a 1920's range that included substantial food and hardlines orientations. Wheel-like they have lost place in the lower

price levels through trading-up, elimination of bargain basements and disappearance of many popular-priced department
stores. The national mass merchants shifted to metropolitan
markets after long entrenchment as suppliers to rural and small
town consumers (a market now again becoming attractive). The
old style semi-surreptitious hardlines discount house, perhaps
a forerunner of the contemporary discount department store,
appealed to a surprisingly affluent audience. Thus the market
array of GAF retailers a half century or so ago was very different from the present one.

Hirschman wouldn't dispute these observations but apparently feels that inherent evolutionary processes have produced the
current market-share allocations. The question is whether the
current condition is the end product or simply a stage in a
rather rapid change process. The theory may turn out to be
more relevant to institutional and customer segmentation, than
to institutional evolution. And since, for example, the Wheel
does not apply in developing countries, perhaps Wadinambiaratchi
(1972) is right in saying that it too is simply an artifact of
a particular industrial evolutionary stage.

Many illustrations support the older evolutionary models,
but they are selective, anecdotal and subject to ill-defined
concepts of such conditions as newness, assortment width,
dominance, maturity and vulnerability. Dating life cycles is
very difficult. Did conventional department stores reach
maturity between 1906 and 1916 when at least forty percent
closed (Brisco 1935), by the crisis of the 1920's (Madison
1976), by 1935 (Barker and Anderson 1935), or after World War
II?

The most serious lack is a good a priori typology of retail
institutions that would force an exhaustive test of any
hypothesized pattern. At present our discussions always concentrate on selected conforming "types" and ignore many other
store varieties. Why don't we try to pattern the small, self-
service checkout grocery stores that mushroomed in the 1920's,
the "job lot" stores of a slightly earlier period, the chain
cigar stores that once appeared on many city street corners, or
the greeting card stores that emerged in the 1960's? We lack
firm rules to determine whether those varieties are "types"
whose histories should help test our theories.

Sadly, the naturalists who might serve as our examplars
have lost control of their own taxonomy. Following Linneas,
Darwin and Huxley they have divided the animate world into king-
dom, phylum, class, order, family, genus, species, subspecies,
variety and population. They now recognize about 5,300 coral
species, 4,800 sponges and 2,000 oysters (Tucker 1979).

Pinder and Moore (1979) suggest an approach to organizational taxonomy for middle-range theorizing which we might apply to retailing types. They recommend recognition of: (1) multiple parameters, so we might classify on the basis of merchandise assortment, customer service method, price level, organizational affiliation, etc.; (2) degree of variation around central tendency, so that department stores might be seen as less homogeneous than convenience food stores; (3) rates of change, so that box stores might be distinguished from more stable types; and most importantly, (4) intra-organization differences so that we might contrast rather than consolidate basement and couturier departments. Applied to all retailing, these suggestions would easily give us far too many categories. But they could be meaningful in the recommended limited range studies, and certainly taxonomy is a major challenge for us.

Improved taxonomy would help increase the models' explanatory and predictive capacities. For example, Berens (1980) cites the typical innovator's capital shortage to explain the low-level entry characteristic of the Wheel. This lack of resources supposedly forces a bare bones market entry. But this explanation rests upon a definition. We tend to call new non-service and low-service stores "new types," while unique high service and luxury stores are viewed as part of the established pattern. Capital limitations are rampant among the transitory trendy little boutiques and luxury shops. There are other difficulties with Behren's explanation, although it merits considerable study. He may be helping to explain, not the Wheel, but the fact that imitators are often more successful than innovators. My own explanation for the Wheel accepts the assumption that most modern retail innovations conserve inputs rather than create new outputs (except suburban shopping centers, machine vending, and probably convenience grocery stores, none of which have conformed to the Wheel) and that market saturation, lost economies of scale and creeping overheads push the firms up the cost and price ladders.

Environmental Determinism

Finally, we should note another way of building macro-theory. Here retailing is seen as result, not cause; as the dependent variable in a world of environmental forces. At its silliest this method merely throws many exogenous variables and some retail trade statistics into a computer and then publishes any correlations that survive a .05 confidence test. In literary history, e.g., McNair and May (1976), the concept may be modified to include mercantile entrepreneurship as a mediating device. Usually, however, the approach is statistical. In thoughtful and meaningful work (Hall, Knapp & Winsten 1961,

Bucklin 1972, Lusch and Ingene 1980) much more complex systems of relations, presumably based on a priori hypotheses, are tested against cross sectional data. The geographic units of analysis may be SMSA's, states or countries, but the aim is to find the full set of factors that cause variations in sales, costs, productivity or structure. Some of Hall's constructions, for example, include willingness to enter the trade (retailer supply) as well as consumer market considerations.

But these studies are very demanding and are not usually replicated. (Bucklin does precede his statistical cross section study with an historical narrative.) Consequently, changing relationships may go unidentified and so any particular model version may be more heuristic than explanatory or predictive. Thus Dawson (1979) notes that Hall, Knapp and Winsten reported a pronounced positive correlation between city size and chain store penetration in the 1950 British census, but that relation- ship no longer exists.

The study of external variables may seem frustrating to management, since business obviously cannot shift population densities or adjust national incomes to modify sales per employee. This is somewhat similar to the Commission of the European Communities' (1978) view of central place theory--use- ful to the planning authorities. But, as noted, such analyses can help corporate planners measure opportunity and performance.

A Two-Faced Final Paradox

This sketchy review notes some, and omits some, seminal work. The foundation is obviously impressive but we are only at the threshold. Besides developing better taxonomies and more knowledge of shopping satisfactions, retail macrotheory should look outward--to the externalities or social impacts, costs and benefits. Simultaneously, retail microtheroy should give renewed attention to how internal information flows and their manipulation (through "loading"--artificial internal overstatements of merchandise cost- and budgeting-devices) affect decision making. Like Janus, retailing theorists must look both ways.

REFERENCES

Adams, Donald Y. (1963), Shonto (Bureau of American Ethnology Bulletin 188). Washington: Smithsonian Institute.

Alderson, Wroe (1957), Marketing Behavior and Executive Action. Homewood, Ill.: Richard D. Irwin.

91

Alexander, Alec P. (1968), "Merchants and the Recruitment of Industrialists," in Markets and Marketing in Developing Enoconomies. R. Moyer and S. C. Hollander, eds. Homewood, Ill.: Richard D. Irwin, 190-208.

Baranoff, Seymour (1965), "Retailing as an Operating System," in Theory in Marketing, 2d Series. R. Cox, W. Alderson and S. Shapiro, eds. Homewood, Ill.: Richard D. Irwin, 154-62.

Barker, Clare and Ira D. Anderson (1935), Principles of Retailing. New York: McGraw Hill.

Berens, John S. (1980), "Capital Requirements and Retail Institutional Innovation--Theoretical Considerations," paper, AMA Marketing Theory Conference, Phoenix, February 10-13.

Brisco, Norris A. (1935), Retailing. New York: Prentice-Hall.

Bucklin, Louis P. (1972), Competition and Evolution in the Retail Trade. Englewood Cliffs, N.J.: Prentice-Hall.

Davidson, W. R., A. D. Bates and S. J. Bass (1976), "The Retail Life Cycle," Harvard Business Review 54 (November-December), 89-96.

Dawson, John A. (1979), The Marketing Environment. New York: St. Martins Press.

Dreesmann, A. C. R. (1968), "Patterns of Evolution in Retail Trade," Journal of Retailing (Spring), 64-81.

Ellsworth, Theodore D. (1976), "Retail Marketing in the USA 1976," Retail and Distribution Management 5 (May-June), 25-37.

European Communities-Commission (1978), The Aspects of Establishment, Planning and Control of Urban Retail Outlets in Europe. Luxembourg: European Community Office for Official Publications.

Fallers, Lloyd (1962), Comments on 'The Lebanese in West Africa,'" Contemporary Problems in Society and History 4 (April), 334-36.

Fishwick, Marshall, ed. (1978), "The World of Ronald McDonald," Journal of American Culture 1 (Summer), 336-471.

Gist, Ronald R. (1968), Retailing: Concepts and Decisions.
New York: John Wiley.

Halbert, Michael (1965), The Meaning and Sources of Marketing
Theory. New York: McGraw Hill, 37-43.

Hall, Margaret, John Knapp and Christopher Winsten (1961).
Distribution in Great Britain and North America. London:
Oxford University Press.

Harris, Leon (1979), Merchant Princes. New York: Harper and
Row, 1-35.

Hirschman, Elizabeth C. (1978), "A Descriptive Theory of Retail
Market Structure," Journal of Retailing 54 (Winter), 29-48.

_____ and Ronald W. Stampfl (1980), "Roles of Retailing in
the Diffusion of Popular Culture: Microperspectives,"
Journal of Retailing 56 (Spring), 16-36.

Hollander, Stanley C. (1978a), "Can We Go Back: The Case of
Farmers Markets," in Research Frontiers in Marketing,
S. C. Jain, ed. Chicago: American Marketing Association,
301-03.

_____ (1978b), "Retailing Research," in Review of Marketing 1978, G. Zaltman and T. V. Bonoma, eds. Chicago:
American Marketing Association, 73-137.

_____ (1980), "Oddities, Nostalgia, Wheels and the Nature
of Retail Evolution," in Competitive Structures in Retail
Markets, R. W. Stampfl and E. C. Hirschman, eds. Chicago:
American Marketing Association, 78-87.

Holton, Richard H. (1953), "Marketing Structure and Economic
Development," Quarterly Journal of Economics 67 (August),
344-61.

Hower, Ralph (1943), History of Macy's of New York. Cambridge,
Mass.: Harvard University Press.

Kizilbash, A. H. and E. T. Carmen (1975-76), "Grocery Retailing
in Spanish Neighborhoods," Journal of Retailing 51
(Winter), 15-21.

Lusch, Robert F. and Charles A. Ingene (1980), "A Theory of
Labor Productivity in Department Stores," in Competitive
Structure in Retail Markets. R. W. Stampfl and E. C.
Hirschman, eds. Chicago: American Marketing Association,
89-107.

MacDonald, Dwight (1952), "White Sales and Aristotle II," The New Yorker 27 (February 9), 39-55.

McNair, Malcolm P. (1958), "Significant Trends and Developments in the Postwar Period," in Competitive Distribution in a Free High-Level Economy, A. B. Smith, ed. Pittsburgh, Pa.: University of Pittsburgh Press.

_____ and Eleanor G. May (1976), The Evolution of Retail Institutions in the United States. Cambridge, Mass.: Marketing Science Institute.

Madison, James B.. (1976), "Changing Patterns of Urban Retailing in the 1920's," Business and Economic History, 2nd Series 5, Paul Useldig, ed. Urbana, Ill.: Bureau of Business and Economic Research, University of Illinois.

Pinder, C. C. and L. F. Moore (1979), "The Resurrection of Taxonomy to Aid the Development of Middle Range Theories of Organizational Behavior," Administrative Science Quarterly 24 (March), 99-118.

Salmon, Kurt Associates (1979), Soft Goods Outlook (December).

Stone, Gregory (1954), "City Shoppers and Urban Identification," American Journal of Sociology 60 (July), 36-45.

Tauber, Edward M. (1972), "Why Do People Shop?" Journal of Marketing 36 (October), 46-49.

Tucker, William (1979), "The Sinking Ark," Harper's 258 (January), 17-27.

Wadinambiaratchi, G. (1972), "Theories of Retail Development," Social and Economic Studies 21 (4), 392-403.

Williams, Robert H., John J. Painter and Herbert R. Nichols (1978), "Policy Oriented Typology of Grocery Shoppers," Journal of Retailing 54 (Spring), 27-42.

A REVIEW OF RETAIL STORE EXPERIMENTS

Benjamin Lipstein
Graduate School of Business Administration
New York University

ABSTRACT

In reviewing retail store experimentation, consideration
is given to the principles of experimental design and those
technical issues which are unique to retail store testing.
The retail store as the experimental unit is discussed as well
as the test variables which have been commonly considered.
The types of measurements as well as the variety of designs
which have been used in retail experimentation are discussed.
Finally, those factors which can disrupt a retail store experiment are identified.

INTRODUCTION

Retail merchants in the management of their business have
always experimented to improve the sales or profitability of
their business. The good retailer intuitively knows that he
must vary his merchandising practices to find that particular
arrangement which will benefit his business. Without the
benefit of scientific experimental design methods, retail
managers have regularly and will continue to rearrange shelf
space, feature new items, offer price leaders, use special
displays, use space or window advertising as well as a host of
other variables to improve the volume and profitability of
their business.

For a variety of reasons, not the least of which has been
the desire of national marketers to improve their position
with retailer and advance sales of their own brands, scientific methods of research in retail experiments have been
widely used over the past thirty years. Singularly, the most
important ingredient added to the testing process in retail
tests has been the use of scientific principles of experimental
design. It is always difficult to establish historically when
and where a methodology was first used. Almost any statement
that one makes about historical precedents is almost certain
to be contradicted by someone else. Notwithstanding this
hazard, some of the earliest work in the application of experimental design to retail store testing is to be found in the
U. S. Department of Agriculture. This flowed from a strong

school of experimental design within the Department and Congressional directives to study ways and means of increasing the sale of various agricultural products. In the years that followed, market researchers in industry and university professors recognized the needs for sound research principles in retail store testing and the contribution which this methodology could make to business enterprise. A very extensive literature over the last thirty years has appeared in the professional journals on the subject. In fact, vastly more work has been done by industry researchers which never appears in print. In this regard, a review of experimental methods in retailing is limited by the published record and one's own personal experience.

The historical review of the subject in this paper will occur only happenstance in referencing a particular principle or method which has been used in the past. The primary objective of this paper is to review the methodology for conducting valid experiments in retail stores. This will involve a discussion of the principles of experimental design, the unit of experimentation and observation, and the kinds of marketing treatments that have been tested. There are a whole variety of measurements that can be made in these investigations, each of which have advantages and limitations. Extraneous and uncontrolled factors have a way of cropping up in the most carefully designed and executed studies. An awareness and anticipation of these disruptive influences can aid in the successful execution of the test. A variety of experimental designs have been used or suggested for the efficient execution of these tests. Some of the more commonly used and valuable designs will be discussed and their contribution to retail efficiency and profitability considered. Lastly, one would be remiss if one did not consider the implications of the universal product code and automatic checkout equipment which is just beginning to appear in food supermarkets.

THE PRINCIPLES OF EXPERIMENTAL DESIGN

The principles of experimental design are well known. R. A. Fisher, considered the founder of modern experimental design contributed his monumental effort in this area almost a half century ago. These basic principles have remained intact and are briefly as follows:

A scientifically conducted experiment must use random processes in the selection of the experimental material or the treatments under consideration must be allocated to the test material on some random basis. Randomness serves two purposes. First, it justifies the use of probability distributions which are the basis of statistical inference. Secondly, an aspect of the random process often overlooked is that the random process of selection or application of treatments has the effect of dispersing unknown and ever present disturbing factors which affect the experiment. The random process distributes these factors over the entire experiment.

A second principle of scientific experimentation is replication. Replication serves two purposes. It provides the basis for variance computation which is critical to statistical analysis and statistical inference. Secondly, by increasing the size of sample the sensitivity of the experiment can be increased.

The third principle is called local control or blocking. This involves arranging the experimental material into homogeneous groupings or blocks so that each treatment is applied to material of a similar kind.

THE RETAIL STORE AS THE EXPERIMENTAL UNIT

While it is self evident that the retail store is the unit of experimental manipulation and the experimental unit, there are still a number of alternatives which one can consider to obtain an efficient experimental design. Rarely is an entire retail store from a sales point of view included in the experiment. More often it is a particular product category, a shelf section, a special display or similar limited area. Duration of time is an integral part of the experimental unit. This enters in two ways, first, how long should the particular treatment, i.e., price, promotion, etc., remain in the store, and secondly, what should the period of observation be. There are many options on duration of measurement. Experiments have ranged from one hour to many months. Statistical efficiency and operational feasibility are a guide in this area.

While the unit of experimentation is the retail store, there are a number of ways in which the experimental unit can be handled in an experiment. There are at least four different ways in which exposure can be achieved. They are monadic exposure, paired comparison, switch-over arrangements and before and after exposure. Each of these methods of exposure have their advantages and limitations.

The monadic use of retail stores involves the use of one stimulus in the particular retail store. This stimulus can be a particular price of a product under examination, a shelf arrangement of merchandise, a single end-of-aisle display or any other single experimental variable. By contrast, in some test situations, one can use the retail store in a paired comparison mode. For example, in considering two alternative pack-on premiums, these promotions could be exposed in the same retail stores in end-of-aisle displays. In experimental design terms the retail store is an experimental block. Both treatment alternatives are exposed within the block. Statistically it has the same properties as paired comparisons as in product testing. As in most paired comparison tests, the dual exposure of stimuli deviate from real world experience. There are important and powerful statistical reasons for considering the paired comparison exposure procedure. Most importantly, in the paired comparison situation, the experimental treatments are compared within the block. Hence, the comparisons are free of block effects or block variation. Since retail stores can differ considerably in many important characteristics which would affect the response to the stimulus, a statistical design which eliminates this source of variation has much to commend it. This use of the retail outlet as the block within the context of a complete block experiment will be discussed below.

The switch-over design is a third method of exposure in retail experiments. In this design, the retail store is exposed on a monadic basis to one particular treatment variation. In the second period, or after a brief waiting time to diminish the effects of the initial treatment, a second treatment is applied to this retail store. Similar rearrangements are carried out with other stores in the experiment. The obvious advantage of the switch-over treatment arrangement is that each store receives two or more treatments. The limitation is the carryover effects or contamination from the previous treatment exposure.

The before and after method of exposure is in some sense a modification of the switch-over treatment approach. The before is viewed as a control followed by the application of the treatment variation. This kind of exposure provides a basis for a study of co-variation.

TEST VARIABLES IN RETAIL STORE TESTS

The retail store can be viewed as a microcosm of the marketing scene. In reviewing the large variety of marketing variables which have been tested in retail stores, it becomes apparent that the classical four p's of marketing—product, price, promotion and place—have all entered into retail store experiments over the past thirty years. Issues of display are equivalent to the factor of place. Pricing studies are self evident. The promotional factor is covered by the advertising and promotional testing. Lastly, the factor of product occurs with the testing of new products and variations in packaging.

The issue of placement of the product within the retail store has occupied a considerable volume of the literature. Retailers as well as national marketers have explored in great depth the placement of merchandise in stores. At perhaps the simplest level is the number of facings per brand. National marketers have fought and are still fighting for additional shelf facings. The published and unpublished experiments have tried to demonstrate the volume and profitability of additional shelf facings. Closely related to number of shelf facings is shelf positions. Marketers have tried to determine the advantages of horizontal versus vertical display of company related products and in the process, have tried to determine the advantages of eye level position as opposed to other shelf positions. Recognizing the limitations of space in retail stores and the fierce competition for shelf facings, national marketers have undertaken shelf space studies and their impact on retail margins to win the support of retailers.

Still within the context of place are the many studies of in-store displays. These run the gamut of end-of-aisle displays to shelf hangers, aimed at increasing areas of selling and sales.

The retail store has proved to be an effective testing ground for evaluating consumer reaction to price. Pricing studies have included testing alternative prices for the introduction of a new product, testing the effect of a change in price of an existing product, the effect of label-off promotions on sales of the brand and even cross branding of products to encourage trial. In most applied situations, the marketer has used the relative performance of different price levels for decision making. In more recent years greater consideration has been given to the issue of price-quantity relationships and price elasticity.

Promotional activities in retail store testing have ranged widely. The effect of trading stamps has been a constant issue of the trading stamp companies in trying to demonstrate the effect of sales volume on the store by distributing trading stamps with purchases. Double stamp days are a regular practice of some retail chains based on extensive testing. In-store advertising has entered into the testing area both for the direct benefit of the retailer as well as paid space for national advertisers. However, most interesting

99

is the evaluation of advertising effort in retail store sales. Here, the work of the Newspaper Advertising Bureau (1977) and the value of a single ad should be noted. However, the most exciting development in recent years is the Universal Product Code and automatic check-out scanners. Some of the work has demonstrated that advertising can have a direct and immediate effect on retail sales.

Finally we have the fourth of the four p's, product. The retail store has been a useful vehicle for testing the introduction of new products and line extensions. This has included such variables as different grinds of coffee and variations in package size.

The retail store has been a critical experimental unit in testing the viability of new packaging for existing products. There have been sufficient disasters in package changes for existing brands to make it mandatory that a new package be store tested. Does the regular buyer of that brand recognize the brand in the new package? Do they think something has been changed in the product content to cause concern with buying the product?

While this is only a brief review of variables which have been tested in retail stores and attempts to cover only the main variables considered, we can be reasonably certain that few if any variables in retailing have been overlooked by the retailer or national marketer in retail store experiments.

TYPES OF MEASUREMENT

In the design of a retail store test there are a number of options in deciding how to measure the results of the experiment. Sometimes this will be dictated by the nature of the retail store experiment. However, often the decision rests with the researcher. In this section we examine the variety of measurement alternatives which may be available in the design of the experiment and the advantages and limitations associated with each. Store audit market share data are perhaps the most common statistics available on retail store activity. Examination of monthly and bimonthly share of market data for individual brands over time gives the impression that market shares and trends are stable slow-moving statistics. This is an illusion. Most store audit market share data are moving averages over one or more months. The bimonthly data of the Nielsen service span a period of almost four months. This is a function of the

mechanics of data collection. In the efficient utilization
of their field force and to produce timely bimonthly reports,
individual store audits are conducted by the field auditors
from January to April for a February/March audit report.
These statistics are essentially moving averages which give
the illusion of great stability in retail sales and market
shares.

In reality, volume of sales and market shares gyrate
wildly from day to day. As every student of retail sales
activity knows, food store sales are substantially higher
on Thursday, Friday, and Saturday than at the beginning of
the week. There are wide fluctuations in retail sales as a
function of the seasons of the year and holidays like Easter
and Christmas.

Volume of retail sales vary substantially by hours of
the day, days of the week, and weeks of the year. This is
not only true for sales volume, but also for market share.
One key to the efficient design of retail store experiments
is to capture this variation in volume of sales and share of
market to the benefit of the experiment rather than leaving it
as a random event which may obscure the issues under investigation. There are often a number of options which the investigator has in deciding on measurement. They are:

Interview of the retail customer before and after
   shopping.
Observation of shopper behavior and actual purchases.
Daily sales of items if automatic check-out facilities
   are available.
Store audits, daily, weekly or monthly volume of sales
   and market share.
Hourly, daily, or weekly shelf disappearance of merchandise.

When the investigation is concerned with shopper intentions and execution, it may be necessary and desirable to
interview the shopper before and after the shopping experience. It is obviously important in the pre-interview to
avoid affecting the shopper as a result of the interview.
Here skillful design of the questionnaire is called for to
obscure the primary purposes of the interview. Shopper
behavior studies would then call for an interview after the
shopping experience. Some interaction effects due to the
pre-interview will always exist. This can be evaluated by
a split design in which some shoppers are interviewed before
and after and some only after the shopping experience. The
difference if any can be ascribed to the pre-interview.

Observation is often a very useful device in retail experiements. When actual shopper behavior in the store is at issue, then observation of their behavior is critical. However, observation is also a very useful and effective procedure for measuring sales volume. In some situations, it is the only effective way in which sales volume and market share can be measured.

Houseman and Lipstein (1960) reported on a retail store experiment involving the movement of apples in supermarkets using the observation technique. Because of the use of dump displays and spoilage, standard audit procedures of opening inventories, purchases and closing inventories were not possible. Observing apple purchases was the most feasible measurement procedure for measuring apple sales. Recognizing that customer traffic and sales volume differ widely by day of the week and hours of the day, a stratification scheme was designed, separating hours into heavy, medium and light traffic periods. A disproportionate sampling of the heavy shopping hours were selected relative to the light and medium traffic periods for observing customer purchases. By this stratification procedure the wide variation in volume of sales from period to period was substantially eliminated from the experiment, increasing the efficiency of the design for the issue under consideration. Since all strata--light, medium and heavy traffic periods--were included in the sample of observations, the between strata variation does not contribute to the experimental variation and error.

Shelf disappearance is still another method of measure-ment. This simply involves the counting of merchandise at the beginning and end of the period of observation. It is of utmost importance that the shelves be fully stocked to avoid an out-of-stock condition. Depending on the speed of move-ment of the merchandise and variation in sales, these observa-tions can be made for a period of an hour, multiples of hours, a day, a week, or longer. The same principles used in the observation technique described above can be used in deciding on the duration of time for measuring shelf disappearance as well as the periods of time to be sampled and observed.

Based upon prior retail experience or actual observation of customer traffic, the time periods can be grouped into strata on the basis of likely volume of sales. A dispropor-tionate sampling procedure is often statistically more desirable. The heavier traffic periods would be sampled more heavily than the medium or light periods. Again the variation between strata (heavy, medium and light) are removed from the experimental variation since all of the strata are sampled and included in the experiment.

102

Store audits are the traditional way in which retail volume and market share have been measured. The traditional store audit involves the taking of an opening inventory of the products in question, recording the purchases by the store or merchandise received, taking a closing inventory and by the simple equation of opening inventory plus purchases minus closing inventory, arriving at sales for the period. The economic as well as statistical advantages are obvious. The investigator need only visit the establishment at the beginning and end of the time period. Total sales volume and market share are readily obtained for as short or as long a time period as one desires. In using the standard audit procedure, the time period and the sample of stores are the statistical issues to be considered. Typically, the retail stores will be grouped into strata on the basis of the retail volume. Each stratum will be sampled, with the high volume strata receiving a disproportionate sample representation. The period of time which the audit will span is a function of the treatments to be observed and measured. For store audit operations, one week is the minimum time period and two months is typically the outside limit. In the case of merchandise testing situations, one week is often operationally most desirable.

There are limitations associated with the standard audit procedure. First and foremost is obtaining retailer cooperation. Aside from overcoming retailer reluctance to cooperate in merchandising tests and auditing procedures in recent years, the cooperation fees required by retailers have been increasing substantially, adding to the increasing cost of these activities. Having obtained retailer cooperation, the next most critical issue is obtaining all purchase records over the audit period. Inadequate or missing purchase records is the most serious shortcoming of standard store audit. Key to a quality audit is an accurate count of inventory. The auditor must locate stock which may be accidently hidden in the dark recesses of the back rooms or basements of retail stores. In any event, when properly executed retail store audits are an outstanding method of measurement for retail store experiments.

Automatic checkout facilities are still in limited distribution. However, as they become more widespread, they become a superlative method of measurement for retail store experiments. With access to these facilities and resultant information, movement of merchandise by category and by brand can be observed for any time period desired. This can be hourly, daily or weekly. The sampling issue disappears since data are available for all time periods. Preliminary reports on the analysis of data from automatic checkout facilities hold out enormous promise of isolating the effects of a large variety of facets which affect the marketing process.

EXTRANEOUS FACTORS WHICH CAN AFFECT
THE RESULTS OF THE EXPERIMENT

The care given in the design of the retail store experiment, the use of monadic exposure vs. paired comparison, the nature of the stimuli or treatment variation, the kinds of observations or measurements and the decisions of the particular experimental design are all intended to control the variation in the experiment and capture it for the benefit of analysis and statistical testing. In spite of all the care exercised in these areas, various problems do arise which can disrupt and distort the results of the experiment. This section of the paper is directed at identifying some of the external factors that can distort the results of the experiment. They require monitoring and, if possible, measurement that can be factored into the final analysis.

The intervention of the sales force in an experiment can be an unfortunate source of distortion. Typically, they should be advised that a special test or experiment is being conducted and told what, if any, role they are to play. Hopefully this will produce the necessary cooperation. Sometimes awareness on the part of the sales force may be interpreted as a situation in which they are being evaluated. This may produce heightened activities on their part which confuse the results. Similarly, there are hazards of not informing them of the test situation. If they stumble on it accidently, they may through shelf stocking, rearrangement of merchandise or other activities, completely destroy the experiment. Most often, the safest route is to advise the sales force of the experiment, explaining the purpose and requesting their cooperation.

Some of the factors that can affect the test are: Sales force intervention, out-of-stock condition, newspaper strike, competition is overstocked, price cutting by competition, competition is out-of-stock, special promotions by competition, competitive change in price, and unusual climatic conditions.

UNIVERSAL PRODUCT CODE AND AUTOMATIC PRODUCT SCANNING

It would be remiss not to discuss the implications of the Universal Product Code and Automatic Check Out Scanners. The technological advantage is clear. Through coding by the manufacturer and automatic scanning of product purchase, a data base of great value is generated. Even with the limited retail store coverage currently available through Nabscan or other facilities, interesting and important observations are being made. The full value and implications of this new technology is yet to be realized. A broader sample coverage of retail outlets and the ability of marketers to introduce test variables and measure their effect will substantially advance our understanding of how these marketing variables affect results at the retail level. All of the principles of experimental design continue to apply. This technology provides almost instantaneous data for any period of measurement desired. It will facilitate identifying the effect of marketing variables with greater ease than ever before.

REFERENCES

Anderson, Evan E. (1972), "Split Plot Design: Measuring Market Share," Journal of Advertising Research, (August), 17-20.

_____ (1979), "An Analysis of Retail Display Space: Theory and Methods," Journal of Business, 52 (January), 103-18.

Audits and Surveys, Inc. (no date), A Discussion of Experimental Designs in In-Store Testing, New York: Audits and Surveys Inc.

Barclay, William D. (1969), "Factorial Design in a Pricing Experiment," Journal of Marketing Research, VI (November), 427-29.

Bennett, Sidney and J. B. Wilkinson (1974), "Price-Quantity Relationship and Price Elasticity Under In-Store Experimentation," Journal of Business Research, (January), 27-38.

Buzzell, Robert D., Walter J. Salmon, and Richard F. Vancil (1965), Product Profitability Measurement and Merchandising Decisions, Boston: Harvard University.

Cairns, James P. (1968), "Suppliers, Retailers, and Shelf Space," Journal of Marketing, 32 (July), 34-36.

Chevalier, Michel (1975), "Increase in Sales Due to In-Store Display," Journal of Marketing Research, XII (November), 426-31.

Cochran, William G. and Gertrude M. Cox (1957), Experimental Designs, New York: John Wiley & Sons, Inc.

Coulson, John S. (1976), "Advertising Payout," Journal of Advertising Research (November).

Cox, Keith K. (1964), "The Responsiveness of Food Sales to Shelf Space Changes in Supermarkets," Journal of Marketing Research, I (May), 63-67.

_____ (1970), "The Effect of Shelf Space Upon Sales of Branded Products," Journal of Marketing Research, VII (February), 55-58.

Curhan, Ronald C. (1974), "The Effects of Merchandising and Temporary Promotional Activities on the Sales of Fresh Fruits and Vegetables in Supermarkets," Journal of Marketing Research, XI (August), 286-94.

_____ (1973), "Shelf Space Allocation and Profit Maximization in Mass Retailing," Journal of Marketing, 37 (July), 54-60.

Doyle, Peter and B. Zeki Gidengil (1977), "A Review of In-Store Experiments," Journal of Retailing, 53, no. 2 (Summer), 47-62.

Frank, Ronald E. and William F. Massey (1970), "Shelf Position and Space Effects on Sales," Journal of Marketing Research, VII (February), 59-66.

Gerhold, Paul E. J. (1976), "How Advertising Pays," Proceedings of the Annual Meeting of the Advertising Research Foundation, New York: Advertising Research Foundation.

Hansen, John R. (1979), "Retail Terminals Mind the Store," Infosystems, 3 (March), 54, 56, 58.

Honomichl, Jack (1979), "New Practices Spur In-Store Research Growth," Advertising Age, (November), 76.

Hoofnagle, William S. (1965), "Experimental Designs in Measuring the Effectiveness of Promotion," Journal of Marketing Research, II (May), 154-62.

Houseman, Earl E. and Benjamin Lipstein (1960), "Observation and Audit Techniques for Measuring Retail Sales," Agricultural Economics Research, 12, no. 3 (July), 61-72.

Hubbard, Charles W. (1969), "The 'Shelving' of Increased Sales," Journal of Retailing, 45, no. 4 (Winter), 75-84.

Klein, Robert L. (1979), "Using Scanner Technology for Market Response Measurement," Proceedings of the 25th Annual Conference of the Advertising Research Foundation, New York: Advertising Research Foundation.

Kotzan, Jeffrey A. and Robert V. Evanson (1969), "Responsiveness of Drug Store Sales to Shelf Space Allocations," Journal of Marketing Research, VI (November), 465-69.

Krueckeberg, Harry F. (1969), "The Significance of Consumer Response to Display Space Reallocation," Proceedings of the American Marketing Association, Series No. 30 (Fall), 336-39.

Lipstein, Benjamin (1967), "Design of Test Marketing Experiments," Journal of Advertising Research, 2-7.

Malec, John (1979), "Ad Testing Through the Marriage of UPC Scanning and Targetable T.V.," 25th Annual Conference of the Advertising Research Foundation, New York: Advertising Research Foundation.

_____ (1979), "New Behavior Scan System Ties Grocery Sales to TV Ads," Marketing News, XIII (September 21), 7.

Neale, Richard L. (1977), "What the Scanner Says to National Advertisers," working paper, Advertising Research Workshop of the Association of National Advertisers.

Newspaper Advertising Bureau, Inc. (1977), Double Dividend, New York: Newspaper Advertising Bureau, Inc.

Partner, James W. (1977), "Looking to Work the Whole Spread, Sharing the Data Base for Operation Payout," 23rd Annual Conference of the Advertising Research Foundation, New York: Advertising Research Foundation.

Peterson, Robert A. and James W. Cagley (1973), "The Effect of Shelf Space Upon Sales of Branded Products: An Appraisal," Journal of Marketing Research, X (February), 103-104.

Pomerance, Eugene (1979), "UPC Symbol Not Delivering Goods," Advertising Age, 56 (February 19), S-6.

Steinber, Sandon A. and Richard F. Yalch (1978), "When Eating Begets Buying: The Effects of Food Samples on Obese and Nonobese Shoppers," Journal of Consumer Research, 4 (March), 243-46.

Woodside, Arch G. and J. Taylor Sims (1974), "Retail Experiment in Pricing a New Product," Journal of Retailing, 3 (Fall), 56-65.

_____, and Gerald L. Waddle (1975), "Sales Effects of In-Store Advertising," Journal of Advertising Research, (June), 29-33.

RETAIL LOCATION THEORY

David L. Huff
University of Texas at Austin

ABSTRACT

Enumerable empirical studies are available that are concerned with markets and market structure. Most of these studies, however, lack a theoretical focus. As a result, the findings of such studies lack generality. This paper presents a
unifying theory that relates directly to the spatial aspects
of retailing.

INTRODUCTION

Spatial economics is concerned with what is where and why
(Hoover 1970). Location theory provides a framework for analyzing alternative locations for particular kings of industries. The theory is not intended to describe the actual distribution of economic activities. Nor, is it intended to predict location patterns. Its purpose is merely to show spatial
tendencies. It provides the necessary basis for interpreting
the complexities of reality.

Theory has been conspicuously absent from most empirical
studies on retail location. As a result, much of the factual
information on this subject lacks generality. In order for
spatial patterns at the retail level to be understood, it is
necessary to match facts with theory.

The purpose of this paper is to review central place theory through the use of micro economics. The approach will
utilize partial equilibrium analysis. That is, after making
certain simplifying assumptions, a few relationships will be
examined in detail. Such an approach should provide empirical
studies of retail location with a better focus for formulating
and testing hypotheses.

CENTRAL PLACE THEORY

Definition

Central place theory is a normative theory indicating the
size, spacing, and number of distribution centers required to
provide goods and services to a dispersed population. The

theory was formulated by Walter Christaller, a geographer (Christaller 1966) and August Lösch, an economist, (Lösch 1954).

Assumptions

The basic assumptions underlying the theory are listed below:
1. An unbounded plain.
2. An even distribution of population.
3. Homogeneous consumers.
4. Homogeneous product.
5. No restrictions to entry or exit.
6. Sellers and buyers possess perfect information.
7. Travel is equal in all directions.

Price to the Consumer

The price of a particular good x to a consumer includes not only the retail selling price p but the transportation costs as well. If m represents the distance from a consumer's place of residence to a store and t is the cost per unit of distance, then, the total price paid by a consumer is $p + mt$. There exists a distance r beyond which the consumer will not travel to buy the good because the total price is too high. These relationships can be seen in Figure 1.

Individual Consumer Demand

Each consumer has a demand curve for good x. As the total price increases, less of the product will be demanded. Further, because of the homogeneity assumption, the demand curve will be the same for all consumers. For example, it can be seen from Figure 2 that if a consumer resides next to the retailer's store, the total price will be p and the consumer will purchase q_0 quantity of the good. If a consumer resides m distance away from the store, the total price will be $p + mt$ and the consumer will purchase q_1 quantity of the good. The shaded area of Figure 2 shows the quantities that the consumer will purchase when transport costs are added to the store price p.

Market Area of the Firm

The demand curve shown in Figure 2 will be the same for all consumers because of the homogeneity assumption. Since travel is equal in all directions, it is possible to calculate the total quantity of good x that will be demanded from the retail store at price p. A demand cone such as the one shown in Figure 3 surrounds the store. This cone is based on the shaded plane of Figure 2. The axes, however, have been reversed. The vertical axis represents the quantities demanded

FIGURE 1

PRICE TO THE CONSUMER IS A FUNCTION OF DISTANCE

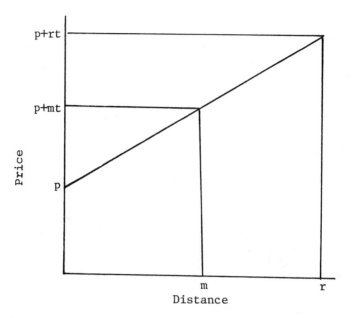

FIGURE 2

INDIVIDUAL CONSUMER DEMAND CURVE

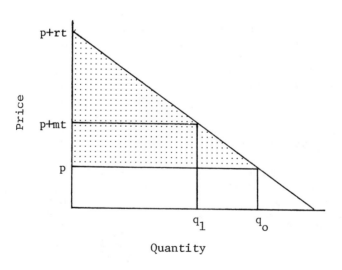

FIGURE 3

GEOGRAPHICAL DEMAND CONE

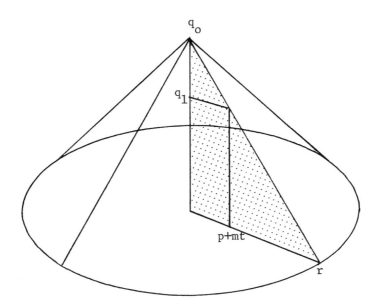

while the horizontal axis designates various total prices of
good $\underline{x}$. The market area of the store is a circle with radius
$\underline{r}$.

The total quantity of good $\underline{x}$ that will be purchased by
consumers residing within the store's market area can be derived as follows (Berry 1967):

$$D_i = S \int_0^{2\pi} [\int_0^{m=r} f(p_i + mt) \, m \, dm] \, d\theta \tag{1}$$

where D_i = total demand of good $\underline{x}$ at price p_i;

      S = population density; and

      p_i = a particular price for good $\underline{x}$.

If D_i is calculated for different store selling prices p_i,
and if these values are plotted in a graph, an aggregate demand
curve can be derived as depicted by DD in Figure 4. If the
marginal revenue (MR), average total cost (AC), and marginal
cost (MC) curves are also graphed, the price that will maximize
the store's profit can be derived. This point is depicted in

111

FIGURE 4

SELLING PRICE YIELDING MAXIMUM PROFIT

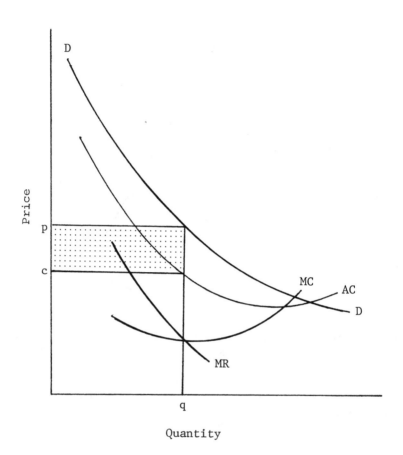

Quantity

Figure 4 where the marginal cost and revenue curves intersect.
Total revenue is the rectangular area bounded by p and q.
Total cost is the area bounded by c and q. The shaded area
shows the difference between these two rectangles. This is
the profit the firm will realize at a store selling price of p.

Hexagonal Market Areas

    The market area of a store, given a selling price of p,
will be a circle with radius r. The number of such circular
market areas will be maximized where the stores form a triangu-
lar hexagonal pattern and each market area is tangential to
six others. These relationships are shown in Figure 5a.

112

FIGURE 5

FORMING HEXAGONAL MARKET AREAS

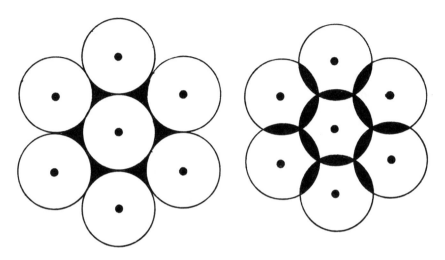

a. Unserved Areas   b. Overlapping Circles

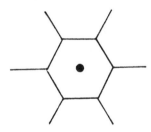

b. Bisecting Areas of Overlap

Ideally, each store would have a circular market area. Consumers located between market areas, however, would be unserved. This can be seen from the shaded areas in Figure 5a. If the circles are moved closer together until the unserved areas are covered, they will overlap (see Figure 5b). The areas of overlap will be bisected and the market areas will become hexagons (see Figure 5c). Other than a circle, a hexagon is the most efficient shape in minimizing the distances travelled by consumers.

The market area of each store is reduced by the outer areas that are severed, total demand is reduced by the loss of consumers who reside in the severed areas. Such a reduction

FIGURE 6

LONG RUN SELLING PRICE

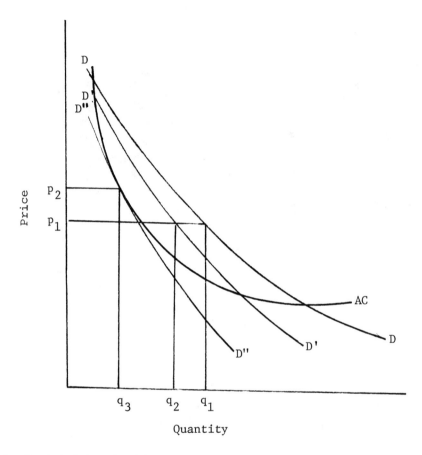

is depicted by the line identified as D'D' in Figure 6.

Maximum Packing

It is assumed that the costs of the firm include the normal rate of return that could be earned in alternative investments. Therefore, the profits shown in Figure 4 are monopoly profits. As long as monopoly profits exist, competition will be intensified. Additional firms will locate and encroach upon each others' market areas. As a result, the market areas will become smaller and total demand will be reduced. The firm's demand curve will continue to shift to the left as long as new firms enter the market. The process of increased packing will continue until the demand curve has shifted so far to the left that it is tangent to the average cost curve. Price at this point of tangency would equal average cost. This can be seen from the curve labeled D"D" in Figure 6.

The ultimate equilibrium results in: (1) the maximum number of sellers of minimum size, (2) a particular good being offered at identical prices, (3) minimum sized hexagonal market areas, and (4) the absence of monopoly profits.

Hierarchy of Market Areas

Normally, a large number of goods and services would be provided to the consumer located on the plain. These goods and services can be rank ordered on the basis of their market radii. Some goods command a wider market radius than others and are thus regarded as higher order goods. The highest order market centers are those that distribute the highest order good and, as a consequence, will have the largest market hexagonal areas. The next sized market centers in the hierarchy will be located exactly at the midpoint between three highest order centers. The good distributed by the next order centers is one whose threshold market area around the new center is a hexagon equal to the hexagonal market area for the same good as provided by each of the three highest order centers. Each lower-level center is located at the midpoint between three higher-order centers. Further, each higher order center is surrounded by six centers of the next smaller size (centers which are located at the corners of a hexagon).

BASIS FOR CLASSIFICATION

Given the assumption and postulates that have been advanced, central place theory reveals how a system of market areas and centers will evolve. It has been shown that such an equilibrium solution results in hexagonal market areas of minimum size and retail firms that are the smallest possible.

No consideration, however, has been given to the welfare aspects of such an equilibrium distribution. From a social point of view, the optimal selling price would not be p_2 as shown in Figure 6 but rather where the marginal cost and average cost curves intersect. Such a solution would not be possible under conditions of monopolistic competition since the demand curve is inelastic. As a consequence, it is impossible for the demand curve to ever be tangential to the lowest point on the average cost curve. The social implications, from the standpoint of allocative efficiency, would be an important area for further study.

In addition, it would be extremely beneficial if existing empirical studies could be classified in terms of the specific aspects of central place theory with which they are concerned. The results of such an undertaking would provide not only an improved basis for classification but it would also indicate the areas where research is needed. Consider, for example, the following questions.

1. What are the ranges for different goods?

2. Do lower-order goods distributed prove higher-order retail centers have greater ranges than those distributed from lower-order centers?

3. Do higher-order centers compete principally among themselves, even for lower-order goods?

4. Do firms possess monopolistic advantages within their respective market areas?

5. Does intensive spatial competition tend to bring about prices that are not in the social interest?

6. What are the threshold requirements for different types of retail firms?

7. To what extent have changes in technology affected the threshold levels of different types of retail firms?

8. How important is the price of a product in affecting an individual's choice of a retail store?

Each of the above questions relates directly to some aspect of central place theory. Further, the list could be expanded. The important thing is that such questions provide the basis for classifying the large number of related empirical studies. Answers to such questions would make it possible to modify the theory in an effort to make it conform more closely to actual conditions.

AN ALTERNATIVE MODEL

An example of a general model that incorporates the main concepts of central place theory was advanced by Huff (Huff 1962). The model depicts consumer choice behavior in terms of Luce's basic choice axiom (Luce 1959). The axiom is:

$$P_T(x) = v(x) / \sum_{y \in T} v(y) \tag{2}$$

where $P_T(x)$ is the probability of an individual choosing alternative $\underline{x}$ from a finite set of T alternatives; T is a subset of some universal set U; and, $v(x)$ is a positive real-valued function v on T.

The basic proposition of this axiom is that choice behavior is best described as a probabilistic, not an algebraic, phenomenon. Thus, the assumption in central place theory that consumers possess perfect information is relaxed. Rather, consumers are assumed to make decisions under conditions of uncertainty. This is due to the fact that products are not assumed to be perfectly homogeneous and that the consumer does not know for sure whether a given store has the desired product. When a consumer reaches a decision between alternative $\underline{a}$ and $\underline{b}$, it is assumed that there is a probability $P(a,b)$ that the choice will be $\underline{a}$ rather than $\underline{b}$ and this probability will generally be different from 0 and 1. The consumer is assumed to be able to evaluate the elements of U along some comparative dimension and to be able to select a finite subset of T alternatives. Furthermore, for situations in which pairwise choice discrimination is imperfect, this choice axiom implies that the ratio of the probabilities of any two choice alternatives is constant and independent of any assumptions about the structure of the set of alternatives.

In addition, the choice axiom complies with the notion of transitivity, i.e., if choice alternative $\underline{a}$ is preferred over $\underline{b}$ and $\underline{b}$ over $\underline{c}$, then, $\underline{a}$ is preferred over $\underline{c}$. While this preference ordering is subject to random fluctuations, it is assumed that such fluctuations are in keeping with the constant probability vector.

The positive real-valued function $\underline{v}$ of $\underline{x}$ that was used initially in the model is:

$$v(j) = A_j^{\gamma} D_{ij}^{-\lambda} \tag{3}$$

where A_j = an attraction index of retail facility $\underline{j}$;

D_{ij} = the accessibility of a retail facility $\underline{j}$ to a consumer located at $\underline{i}$; and

γ, λ = empirically determined parameters.

The probability that a consumer located at $\underline{i}$ will choose to shop at retail facility $\underline{j}$ for a particular product or group of homogeneous products is:

$$P_{ij} = A_j^{\gamma} D_{ij}^{-\lambda} \Big/ \sum_{j=1}^{n} A_j^{\gamma} D_{ij}^{-\lambda} \qquad\qquad (4)$$

The quotient derived by dividing A_j^{γ} by D_{ij}^{λ} is regarded as the perceived utility of retail facility j by a consumer located at $\underline{i}$. Square footage of selling space is often used as a surrogate measure for the attraction variable A_j. Travel time, road and straight-line distance, and travel costs are measures that have been used for the accessibility variable D_{ij}. Once again, another assumption of central place theory has been relaxed--travel is equal in all directions. D_{ij} makes it possible to account for actual conditions of accessibility. The notion that consumers will travel farther to buy goods at larger centers is certainly in keeping with central place theory.

The parameter associated with a variable reflects the sensitivity of the probabilities with respect to that variable. A comparison of the values of these parameters for different types of shopping trips is particularly meaningful. Various estimation procedures have been employed to estimate parameters of non-linear models. In general, the procedures involve specifying some initial value for one of the parameters and then calculating a value for the other using some efficient search routine. This iterative procedure is continued until the lowest sum of squared differences is reached between the actual and expected number of consumers shopping at a specified set of retail facilities.

By multiplying the probability values by various constants, it is possible to derive expected values, e.g., number of customers, value of purchases, etc. Thus, the assumption of homogeneous consumers can be relaxed to reflect different consumption propensities which is a function of socioeconomic differences among consumers.

A consumer's perceived utility of a retail facility is unquestionably determined by a myriad of factors. Equation (4), however, specifies only two variables even though these variables are regarded as surrogates for a number of different variables. While other variables could be included in the model, there is some difficulty in estimating the parameters associated with such variables. Furthermore, the techniques traditionally used in estimating the parameters do not assure that a global maxima or minima will be obtained nor are the statistical properties of the estimates known. Due to the non-linear formulation of the model most researchers believed that the parameters could not be estimated by standard econometric

118

methods. However, recently Nakanishi and Cooper demonstrated that the parameters can be estimated using least squares (Nakanishi and Cooper, 1974). A generalization of equation (4.0) with respect to consumer spatial behavior is as follows:

$$\pi_{ij} = \frac{\prod\limits_{k=1}^{q} x_{kij}^{\beta_k}}{\left(\sum\limits_{j=1}^{m} \prod\limits_{k=1}^{q} x_{kij}^{\beta_k}\right)} \tag{5}$$

where: π_{ij} = the probability that a consumer located at i will choose a retail facility j;

X_{kij} = the kth of q variables describing a retail facility j in terms of a consumer located at i;

β_k = the sensitivity of π_{ij} with respect to variable k; and

m = the number of retail facilities.

After making a log transformation and rearrainging terms, the model is of the form:

$$Y_{ij} = \sum\limits_{k=1}^{q} \beta_k A_{kij} + E_{ij} \tag{6}$$

where:

$Y_{ij} = \log\left(\dfrac{\pi_{ij}}{\pi_i}\right)$ and π_i is the geometric mean of the m different probabilities corresponding to each of the consumers;

$Z_{kij} = \log\left(\dfrac{X_{kij}}{\tilde{X}_{ki}}\right)$ and $\tilde{X}_{ki}$ is the geometric mean of the m different values of X_{kij} describing the retail facilities in terms of variable k for a consumer located at i; and

E_{ij} = the difference between the model estimates for Y_{ij} and the actual values for Y_{ij}.

Thus the original two-variable model can be extended to
q variables and the parameters associated with these variables
can be estimated using least-squares techniques.

The probability values stemming from the model can be
mapped as a continuous distribution. A probability surface
can be constructed that is analogous to the three dimensional
demand cone in central place theory. The intersection of like
probability contours between each pair of retail firms produces a locus of points. Such lines can be interpreted simply
as curves upon which any given individual is indifferent between two retail firms. Even though the isoprobability contours about a retail firm may not be circular, the lines of
equilibrium are always circles or parts of circles (Gambini
1966). It is interesting to note that if the spatial arrangement of retail firms is in the form of equilateral triangles,
the lines of equilibrium will form hexagons. In addition, by
stratifying retail firms by size and deriving lines of equilibrium between them, then overlays can be made to show hier-
archical effects (Huff 1979).

REFERENCES

Berry, Brian J.L. (1967), Geography of Market Centers and
    Retail Distribution, Englewood Cliffs, N.J.: Prentice-
    Hall, Inc., p. 61.

Cristaller, Walter (1966), Central Places in Southern Germany,
    translated by E. W. Baskin, Englewood Cliffs, N.J.:
    Prentice-Hall, Inc.

Gambini, Raymond (1966), A Computer Program for Calculating
    Lines of Equilibrium Between Multiple Centers of Attrac-
    tion, Lawrence, Kansas: Center for Regional Studies,
    University of Kansas.

Hoover, Edgar M. (1970), "The Partial Equilibrium Approach,"
    in: Robert D. Dean, William H. Leahy and David L. McKee,
    Editors, Spatial Economics, New York: The Free Press,
    p. 3.

Huff, David (1962), "A Probabilistic Analysis of Consumer Spa-
    tial Behavior," in: W. S. Decker (Ed.), Emerging Concepts
    in Marketing, Chicago: American Marketing Association.

Huff, David (1979), "Ireland's Urban System," Economic Geogra-
    phy, Vol. 55, No. 3.

Lösch, August (1954), The Economics of Location, translated by
W. H. Woglom and W. F. Stolper, New Haven: Yale University Press.

Luce, R. D. (1959), Individual Choice Behavior, New York: John
Wiley & Sons.

Nakanishi, M. and Cooper, L. G. (1974), "Parameter Estimation
for a Multiplicative Competitive Interaction Model--
Least Square Approach," Journal of Marketing Research,
Vol. 11.

Segal, David (1977), Urban Economics, Homewood, Illinois:
Richard D. Irwin, Inc., pp. 28-30.

NEW REALITIES OF RETAIL MANAGEMENT

Robert F. Lusch, University of Oklahoma, Norman
Ronald W. Stampfl, University of Wisconsin, Madison

ABSTRACT

Due to drastic changes that occurred in the retail environment during the 1970's and the expected continuation of many of the underlying factors causing these changes throughout the 1980's, retail managers must confront a set of new management realities. To complement this new set of management realities, retail managers will need new theories and conceptual frameworks in order to properly manage their organizations in the future. Consequently, the purpose of this paper is to review the old and new realities and to suggest needed areas of theory development and application.

INTRODUCTION

As the 1960's became history for U.S. retailers, they embarked upon a decade which was to shatter many of their assumptions about the socioeconomic environment in which they functioned, and worse, obsolete many of the traditional, established modes of thought which had served them well in the post-war period. The past realities (Berry 1980) of low inflation, low cost energy, solid and continuing growth in GNP, a growing population, high consumer confidence, expanding markets and easy access to capital were changing quickly. As U.S. retailers entered the 1980's, they were increasingly convinced that the trends of the 1970's, however disheartening, were likely to be the realities of the 1980's.

The large, professionally managed retailer, had by the end of the 1970's succeeded in simultaneously convincing: (1) the consumer that it could deliver maximum value for dollar spent; and (2) the manufacturer that it could deliver huge amounts of purchasing power or market share. This was an ideal position. But the new realities hint that retailers may quickly lose the stature with consumers and the power with manufacturers that increasingly became theirs in the turbulent 1970's unless they clearly rethink how they will manage the "basics" of their business.

The purpose of this paper is to identify those changes we see permanently crystallizing in the retail environment. Identification of these changes will assist in revealing how the old realities and/or assumptions of retail management are no longer appropriate and, therefore, why many existing theories of retail management are no longer timely. Consequently, the retail manager will need several new theoretical frames of reference. We shall consider this need in the managerial areas of: (1) capital; (2) human resources; (3) the business cycle; (4) market share management; and (5) profit management.

CAPITAL MANAGEMENT

In mid 1975 Business Week estimated that industry in the U.S. would face a $4.5 trillion capital shortfall by 1985 (Business Week 1975). This estimated shortfall was based on the assumption that the U.S. wanted to remain competitive in world markets and that the federal government would continue deficit financing of its activities and thus place a continued drain on sources of private capital. Whether the $4.5 trillion was an accurate reflection of the severity of the situation or not, the actual facts in the late 1970's indicated the price of capital was high and the supply of readily available capital was tight. By the close of the 1970's the consensus of retail analysts was that the cost of capital for most chain store retailers throughout the first half of the 1980's would be in the 9-12% range. In short, capital had become very expensive by conventional retail standards. For instance it was not uncommon for retailers in the 1950's or 1960's to be able to borrow capital in large quantities at a cost of 4-6%.

The Old Reality
The old management reality in retailing regarding capital management was that capital was readily available, easy to obtain and inexpensive. In addition, the impact of capital costs and leverage upon return on investment was poorly understood by retailers and therefore relegated to the controller's office. It was something a merchant considered unimportant. For example, the composite leverage ratio in 1950 (total assets ÷ net worth) for U.S. retailers was a mere 1.6 times (Internal Revenue Service 1952). Because capital was easy to obtain retailers tended to place heavy emphasis on engineering an attractive income statement while placing little emphasis on balance sheet management. Predictably, key income statement ratios such as the gross margin (gross profit ÷ sales) and net profit margin (net profit ÷ sales) received inordinate attention. Marketing efforts gained in importance as merchants concentrated their efforts on building sales volume to "drive" the income statement. Vendor relations, once the pleasantries were removed, became a search for higher gross margins which ultimately led to the narrowing of merchandise assortments by traditional generalists such as department stores and the broadening of

123

assortments by traditional specialists such as supermarkets. The emphasis upon income statement management in the post war period utlimately helps explain such phenomena as: (1) the emergence of the low margin discounter (expense reduction); (2) the emergence of the specialized chain (unique assortments yielding atypically high gross margins); and (3) the coming of intensive intertype competition for market share in the 1980's.

The New Reality
    By 1976 it was clear that retailers were becoming more sophisticated in capital management and were taking advantage of past easy access to capital, as evidenced by a composite industry leverage ratio of 2.5 times (Federal Trade Commission 1976). By the end of the 1970's retailers began to accept capital scarcity as a new reality and serious attention to dual-track income statement and balance sheet management began to become part of the strategic thinking of progressive retailers. Merchants learned that the assets portrayed in the balance sheet (only part of which was equity) produced the sales shown on the income statement and that the trichotomy of profit margin, asset turnover and leverage produced total profitability as measured by return on net worth-RONW (McCammon and Hammer 1974). This approach--commonly referred to as the strategic profit model-- shows the retailer its return on total assets without regard to who provided the capital (owners or creditors) and also the return on only the capital provided by the owners (net worth). Consequently the model provides two useful standards of capital management: (1) return on assets; and (2) return on net worth.

New Theoretical Needs
    Our ultimate purpose in reviewing the old and new realities of retailing is to point out that because of the new realities retailers have a strong need for new theories on how to manage a retail enterprise. Our discussion of capital management reveals for example that retailers would welcome more theoretical models focusing on working capital management, shifting of channel functions to reduce capital inputs and related impacts upon channel relations, dividend payout models, and liquidity management. Retail academicians that properly incorporate these areas into their theories should be well received by retail managers.

HUMAN RESOURCE MANAGEMENT

    Labor in the U.S. generally became increasingly disenchant- ed during the turbulent 1970's. Younger workers were increas- ingly drawn from a highly educated population socialized to believe there was more to life than work and a career. The life-style customer that retailers increasingly sought in the

1970's through market segmentation strategy has become the life-style employee available for hire in the 1980's. This type of person is simultaneously experiencing the impact of inflation on purchasing power and boredom from day-to-day routine at a job and is turning to life-style rewards as major life objectives. The "organization man" of the 1950's is gone. The un-committed worker has replaced him. In principle, work is increasingly becoming a means to an end. The retailer that fully recognizes this will not only market properly to his customers but will recruit, train, develop and place (and retain) his employees properly. To realize that the new realities affect capital resource management but to ignore their impact upon human resource management is the ultimate folly since the wrong people using the right capital cannot succeed.

The Old Reality

Throughout the history of 20th century U.S. retailing, top retail executives believed that the jobs and career opportunities that they provided employees with were fulfilling. They felt that the retail job or career--challenging, uncertain, and dramatic--should provide fulfillment. They believed that the job or career was the lifestyle and that employees should become totally immersed in their work and design their entire life around their job or career. Employees that conformed were promoted and deviants were scorned. Turnover was high but it was the employee's fault--s/he was not "right for retailing."

Operating under this old reality the appropriate focus was on how much productivity retailers could get from each employee--i.e., sales per employee, profit per employee or dollar sales per payroll dollar. The focus was on what the employee could do for the retailer. Throughout most of the 20th century this orientation served business in general--and retailers in specific--quite well.

The New Reality

The days of the job being the lifestyle are rapidly passing us by. Jobs and careers are rapidly becoming the means to the end. Although disheartening to many aging retailers, young people's values today often place career tracking as secondary and lifestyle as primary. In the future the job or career will have to fit the lifestyle and not vice versa.

The new reality implies that the output of retail employment is not sales or profit (these become the managerial constraints); rather it is satisfaction of the employee. Retailers need to engineer jobs to create satisfaction and need fulfillment while at the same time insuring that a link exists between employee satisfaction and corporate sales and/or profit. But the retailer's initial focus must be on employee satisfaction

and need fulfillment or the ulitmate ROI goal of the retailer
will be jeopardized by increasing turnover of a decreasingly
skilled and motivated pool of employable people. Ultimately,
people produce profit and the wrong people simply cannot produce the "right" results.

New Theoretical Needs
     The preceding suggests that the retailer requires a theory
of human motivation, development and reward which combines life-
style and job compatibility and which recognizes the personal
goals of employees as worthwhile. The traditional management
literature dealing with such areas as job enrichment, partic-
ipatory management and employee motivation must be translated
for the retail environment of the future. The challenge for
the retail vice president of human resources in the coming decade will be to combine the lifestyle needs of employees with
the financial imperatives of a business existing in a highly
competitive environment. Fortunately, the increasing profes-
sionalization of retail management over the past several decades will support this new orientation.

MANAGEMENT OF THE BUSINESS CYCLE

     From the early 1950's through the late 1960's executives
in the U.S. became accustomed to relatively modest swings in
the business cycle. Throughout most of this period most sectors in the U.S. economy, including retailing, were growing at
a relatively constant and predictable pace. Forecasting and
planning based upon linear extrapolation worked surprisingly
well. Unfortunately, during this time frame new executives did
not learn how to manage under wide swings in the business cycle.
They acquired the skills for managing growth but obtained little
experience in managing during recession and recovery. Thus as
these executives were greeted by the turbulent 1970's many were
unprepared.

The Old Reality
     Retail executives were no different than other executives
in the U. S. in regard to understanding the business cycle. It
became perceived as steady and predictable. Next season's inventory was an extrapolation of last year's inventory. New
store expansion was based upon a projection of population and
income trends. This type of behavior worked well because real
dollar sales tended to grow at a constant 3-4% per year. If a
slight downturn was encountered it was likely short-lived and
thus if a mistake was made it was shortly covered over by future sales growth. There was a "management cushion" provided
by real growth in those factors nearest a retailer's heart--
population, disposable income and credit.

126

During the 1950's and 1960's retail executives could fairly well manage the effects of the business cycle by monitoring two ratios--(1) average days of inventory on hand, and (2) average age of accounts receivable. In the case of these ratios becoming too high during a slight recession it was relatively easy to borrow short term capital at a low cost from the bank to keep the retailer liquid for a few months. It is fair to say that the complexities of managing over the business-cycle were not all that extreme in comparison to the problems encountered in the 1970's.

The New Reality
The 1970's brought forth what McCammon et al. (1976) have referred to as a roller coaster economy. The business cycle became more compressed and the swings more dramatic. At the same time due to high inflation consumers reduced their rate of savings and continued to aggressively spend at high levels hoping to avoid higher future prices. The retailer could not judge consumer purchase intentions with any confidence and thus it was often difficult for the retailer to identify what stage the business cycle was in. The new reality became that the business cycle was unpredictable, turbulent and often unidentifiable.

As a consequence of the new reality of the business cycle, retail executives need to devote more time to analysis of the business cycle and to determining the appropriate merchandise response. Retail executives also need to recognize that downturns could potentially be lengthy and severe. They need to recognize downside risks and to consistently remain as flexible as possible in regard to personnel scheduling, inventory reorder potential and long term commitment to capital expenditures.

Retailers will need to monitor more than days of inventory on hand and the age of accounts receivable. They will need to develop and monitor defensive ratios. Defensive ratios show how well a retailer can defend its existence in a recession. One such ratio is (cash + accounts receivable + inventory) ÷ (average daily cash expense). This simple ratio measures survival days for the retailer. In effect, it asks "if sales dropped significantly, how long could the retailer survive?" It also assumes current assets are convertible to cash at full value. If not, survival days must be deflated. We believe that during recession, recovery and growth the retailer should manage survival days and not strictly days of inventory or age of accounts receivable. Furthermore, not only must assets be differentially managed over the business cycle but also average daily expenses. During recession, survival days should be programmed at a comfortable margin; during recovery, survival days can be relaxed; and during growth, survival days

can be kept at a minimum. Obviously this implies that the retailer is able to forecast with some accuracy the stages of
recession, recovery and growth.

It would appear that most retailers must also consider
the possibility of temporary operational consolidation, limited
hours/days of operation or even temporary closings as viable
responses to conditions underlying a low "survival day" ratio.
This will be particularly true for retailers who have "given
away" their countercyclical or basic businesses during less
turbulent times. For example, many department stores have
traded-up to such a level that they sell only ego-intensive
non-necessities to recession vulnerable upper middle class
consumers on credit and through merchandising methods which
imply large mark-ups to cover large operating expenses. To
extend survival days, this type of retailer should consider
how the store might be operated with only certain floors or
departments functioning. Another example may involve discount
or supermarket chains staggering the days or hours of operation
for their various stores in a city.

New Theoretical Needs
    Retailers presently have no comprehensive theory on how to
manage the basics of retailing under recession, recovery and
growth. Consequently this represents a theoretical and research
frontier. Some specific areas that we feel offer considerable
promise are as follows--

        ·break-even reduction models,
        ·portfolio management and the business cycle,
        ·contingency planning models,
        ·adaptive control planning models,
        ·patronage models based on flexible "store
         availability."

                    MANAGEMENT OF MARKET SHARE

From the 1950's through the 1960's markets in the U.S.
were generally expanding. As a result a firm could increase
its sales while at the same time experiencing a decline in
market share. Shrinking market share fostered relatively
little managerial concern as long as sales were growing at an
adequate pace.

During the 1970's, markets of all types began to mature as
the total U.S. economy began to experience slow and often negative rates of real growth. Inflation initially masked the
sales volume effect for the less perceptive retailer but ultimately it became clear that a decline in market share often

128

became synonomous with a drop in sales. Similarly, growth in
sales frequently implied a gain in market share at the expense
of another firm's market share. This development created a
major struggle for market share in many U.S. markets and is
certain to intensify in the 1980's (McCammon, et al., 1980).

The Old Reality

Because most retail markets were growing, retailers in
the 1950 to 1970 time frame generally were not overly concerned
with market share. As the growth of retail markets slowed in
the 1970's retailers began to focus considerable attention on
protecting their market share in their particular line-of-trade.
A retailer's competitors were viewed as other retailers in the
same geographic area operating in the same line of trade. For
example, a popular measure of competitive intensity was line of
trade square feet per geographic area divided by households in
the geographic area.

The New Reality

The old reality of viewing competition and market share
as line-of-trade specific is no longer appropriate. Retailers
need to recognize that, ultimately, they are all competing for
limited consumer spending power. The new reality is that
retailers must protect their share of trade area purchasing
power. Therefore, the most appropriate measure of competitive
intensity in retailing is total retail purchasing power in a
geographic area divided by total retail square feet in a
geographic area. This ratio basically captures the demand for
retail facilities in an area divided by the supply of retail
services. The higher the ratio the less intense the competition among retailers and vice versa. Basically, we are arguing
that when markets are not growing that retailers, regardless
of their line of trade, are all competing for the same potential
purchasing power in a geographic area. Admittedly, this takes
the threat of inter-type competition to its ultimate limits
but the consumer lifestyles of the 1970's have clearly demonstrated consumer expenditure flexibility between seemingly
non-competing retailers when traditional census classifications
are utilized. For example, if in 1965 a consultant would have
told a major supermarket chain executive that his real competition for marginal increases in sales volume in 1975 would be
fast food chains, the consultant might well not have been paid.
Or, what of the young secretary that budgets twenty dollars
for a week of luncheons but decides to go to the disco or buy
a new blouse and skip lunch this week? Or the stereo shop that
would have sold a full system if Bob had not seen the "Ski the
Rockies This Weekend" promotion by a local travel agency? It
is this type of consumer flexibility and the lack of traditional
expansion potential confronting the aggressive merchants of the
1980's that will push all retailers to regard the protection

of their share of total trade area purchasing power as one of
the first imperatives of the new managerial realities.

Finally, an intriguing strategic possibility for expanding market share is to reconceptualize "the store" periodically,
rename and refixture it and thereby reposition its market image.
Brand managers in autos and cigarettes have phased in and out
a variety of brands of generic products during the past two
decades. Does the life style consumer really care if the store
has a history or a future any more than the buyer of a Ford
Granada cared that two years earlier the car was called Torino?
It would appear that "store life" must be minimally planned at
a few years duration but that longevity is no longer a prereq-
uisite to market share success.

New Theoretical Needs

The intensified struggle to capture a significant share
of a trade area's purchasing power will force retailers to
look for new frameworks for obtaining a significant competitive
advantage. Retail theorists might therefore find attempts to
build and/or refine theories in the following areas quite
worthwhile--

- models or theories of free form and divertive
  competition,
- value added strategy models,
- incremental positioning models,
- space utilization models,
- life style segmentation models,
- marginal disposable incomes expenditure models
  at different life cycle stages,
- patronage models not related to store loyalty,
  i.e., can stores have limited, planned life
  spans?

PROFIT MANAGEMENT

Executives have been quite comfortable with using conventional accounting statements as tools to manage profits. The
most popular conventional accounting statements have been the
income statement, balance sheet and sources and uses of funds
statement. All of these statements are constructed using
historical cost data. As long as a retailer's input prices are
stable over time then historical cost accounting statements
are reasonable vehicles for profit management.

The Old Reality

Most U.S. retailers through the late 1960's used historical cost accounting statements to alert themselves to the

quantity of profits they generated. Often these dollar profits were related to other monetary aggregates such as total dollar sales, assets or dollars of equity or net worth. In most respects the higher the profit measure the better performance was thought to be. In short, targets of performance were phrased in terms of high dollar profits or high profit ratios such as return on sales or return on assets.

The New Reality

With the high rates of inflation that were experienced in the 1970's and the expected inflation in the 1980's the old reality of maximizing the quantity of profits as measured by historical accounting statements is no longer appropriate. In fact plans to manage profits based only on the information presented in these outmoded statements are plans for disaster.

The new reality of profit management in retail enterprises needs to be to manage the quality of profits as measured by current value financial statements and current value accounting techniques (Westerfield 1980). The quantity of profits are no longer the best indicators if prices are rapidly rising. The quality of profits however is obtained by more than just adjusting historical cost accounting methods for rising prices. A subjective judgment also enters into the assessment of quality of profits. Specifically, the retail manager must ask him/herself if a dollar of profits in one store or in one merchandise line is more valuable than in another. This would involve a variety of subjective judgments on such things as: (1) the predictability of profits in each area; (2) the stability of profits; and (3) the long run profits in each area.

New Theoretical Needs

Once again we see, because of a shift from the old to the new reality, that retail managers need new theories and/or models. Some general directions in which retail theorists might direct their efforts are as follows:

- decision making models using current value vs. historical cost data,
- models of subjective assessment of the quality of profits,
- theories of executive information processing in an inflationary and turbulent environment,
- theories of stockholder and market response to current value vs. historical accounting statements.

CONCLUDING COMMENTS

Our review of the new and old realities of retail management has resulted in the development of a portfolio of new theoretical needs for the 1980's retail manager. A careful review of these theoretical needs should help to point out that

the 1980's retail manager will need theories of employee motivation, consumer behavior, financial planning, resource utilization, channel behavior, economic cycles, and competitor behavior as well as a host of others. In principle the old reality of the retail manager being a marketer is questionable.
Rather the new reality must become that the retail manager is
a business manager. He or she must manage markets, assets,
profits, people, cycles, and market share simultaneously and
interdependently if ROI goals of the future are to be met.

REFERENCES

Berry, Leonard (1980),"The New Consumer," in Competitive Struc-
ture in Retail Markets: The Department Store Perspective,
Ronald W. Stampfl and Elizabeth Hirschman, eds., Chicago:
American Marketing Association, 1-11.

Business Week (1975),"Capital Crisis: The $4.5 Trillion America
Needs to Grow," (September 22), 42-115.

Federal Trade Commission (1976), Quarterly Report on Manufacturing, Mining and Trading Corporations, Washington, D.C.:
U.S. Government Printing Office.

Internal Revenue Service (1952), Corporate Income Statistics,
Washington, D.C.: U.S. Government Printing Office.

Lusch, Robert F. and James M. Kenderdine (1978),"A Frame of Reference for Managing Working Capital in Retailing, International Journal of Physical Distribution 8, 337-345.

McCammon, Bert C.Jr., and William L. Hammer (1974), "A Frame of
Reference for Improving Productivity in Distribution," Atlanta
Economic Review (September-October), 9-13.

McCammon, Bert C.Jr.,Robert F. Lusch and Bradley T.Farnsworth
(1976), "Contemporary Markets and the Corporate Imperative:
A Strategic Analysis for Senior Retailing Executives," paper
presented at the Grad. School of Bus. Admin., Harvard Univ.

McCammon, Bert C.Jr., Jack J. Kasulis and Jack a Lesser (1980),
"The New Parameters of Retail Competition: The Intensified
Struggle for Market Share," in Competitive Structure in
Retail Markets: The Department Store Perspective, Ronald W.
Stampfl and Elizabeth Hirschman, eds., Chicago: American
Marketing Association, 108-118.

Westerfield, W. U. (1980), "Don't Kill the Messenger,"
Chain Store Age Executive (February), 10.

CONSUMER PERCEPTIONS OF PRODUCT VALUE

Joseph Barry Mason, The University of Alabama
Elizabeth Goldsmith, The University of Alabama

ABSTRACT

Values theory as developed by Rokeach offers a conceptually rich paradigm for exploring the forces influencing consumer perceptions of product value. This paper highlights the hypothesized nature of such relationships.

Marketing researchers have long recognized that values play an important role in consumer buying patterns. Some persons go so far as to say that marketers accord an almost "motherhood" status to the idea that values strongly influence consumption behavior (Vinson & Munson 1976). Yet, few studies have attempted to specify the relations between consumption behavior and value orientation (Scott & Lamont 1974). The early work of Irving White is an exception (White 1966). Donald Vinson has observed that the study of values in influencing purchasing behavior has been largely atheoretical and unscientific (Vinson 1978). Is this criticism justified? What, in fact, do we know about the role and impact of values on consumer behavior and more specifically the perception of value in products?

VALUES THEORY

Philosophers provided much of the original writing on the concept of human values. Their conceptualizations are so esoteric, however, that it has been difficult to apply them directly to such fields of study as marketing. Marketers instead have found more fruitful possibilities for application in marketing under value theories posited by such noted psychologists as Maslow, Piaget, and Rokeach (Clawson & Vinson 1978).

Values are deeply internalized, personal feelings that direct action. In terms of products, something is valuable if it is highly regarded, prized or in some way has worth. What constitutes good value is highly specific to the individual and to the product. What people see as "good value" is linked to their personal value system which can be termed their value orientation. These generalized value orientations can be passed from generation to generation. In a study of 360 families linked by three generations, 120 grandparent families,

120 parent families, and 120 young married families, Hill et al. found much agreement in values orientation across the three generations (Hill 1970). People project their values in their perceptions of products. A person learns what constitutes good value from one's own family and other reference groups and by one's own purchasing trial and error (Stein & Stampfl 1980; Stampfl 1978). What is less obvious is how can values be most accurately assessed and used for an understanding of consumer perception of value in products.

The most extensive investigations of the structure and dynamics of personal value systems by marketers and the relationships of these systems to product choice has been research with value expectancy models based on cognitive theory. Most of the work, however, has concentrated on the prediction of brand preference and has used product attributes instead of generalized values (Darden 1980). While product attributes are appropriate for the problem of efficient prediction of brand appeal, they do not provide an understanding of which personal values underlie the motivation to respond favorably or unfavorably to specific products or promotions (Scott & Lamont 1974).

Other than a few isolated studies discussing changes in national values, research in marketing with few exceptions (Bither & Miller 1969) has thus been in context of the expectancy-value-attitude models of Rosenberg and Fishbein (Vinson, Scott & Lamont 1979). As observed, however, "the expectancy-value approach has been useful in predicting brand choice but does not explain why consumers differentially evaluate product attributes and thus prefer one brand to another." (Vinson, Scott & Lamont 1977, p. 45). Values may be the key to the "why" question.

Recent research has shown, for example, that personal values are factors which are useful for explaining differences in consumption behavior between particular groups of people (Vinson, Munson & Nakanishi 1977), and which may offer a more stable framework for analysis than expectancy value models. Walter Henry found that value dimensions, in a study of the cultural orientations within American society, correlated with the ownership of generic automobile categories (Henry 1976). Similarly, Parker Lessig found that the flow of influence was from values to attitudes toward product attributes to brand preference (Lessig 1975).

A variety of value inventories exist. The Hill three generational study, for example, used the Cognitive Value Scales developed by Orville Brim and his associates at the Russell Sage Foundation (Brim 1962). This scale investigates the concepts of fatalism, impulsivity, pessimism and time orientation; Hill applied it to the acquisition of the family's durable goods inventory. Probably the most well-known values inventory has been developed by Milton Rokeach. The Rokeach value survey has been used in a variety of studies in recent years to investigate the role of values in the evaluation of product attributes (Scott & Lamont 1974), product preferences (Vinson, Scott & Lamont 1977), market segmentation (Vinson & Munson 1976), and in evaluating the structural composition of a consumer's value-attribute system (Vinson & Nakanishi 1976).

The Rokeach work in values identification has been subjected to rigorous conceptual and analytical evaluation over the years. Thus, as observed by James Carman: "It is not true that the Rokeach values survey is just another attempt to measure values that is on thin ice. It has had an incredible amount of testing in a wide variety of applications . . . Rokeach provides a framework and a measure of values that are applicable in anthropology, sociology, psychology and consumer behavior"(Carman 1978).

Rokeach believes that the self-concept is the element most stable in consumer's values. Specifically, "The functions served by a person's values are to provide him with a comprehensive set of standards to guide actions, justifications, judgments, and comparisons of self and others and to serve needs for adjustment, ego defense and self-actualization. All these diverse functions can merge into a single, overriding, master function, namely, to help maintain and enhance one's total conception of self"(Rokeach 1968; Rokeach 1973).

The connection between self-concept and buying behavior has been empirically demonstrated in a variety of studies. Research has shown, for example, that a consumer tends to buy brands similar to his or her self-perceptions (Dolich 1969; Grubb & Grathwohl 1969; Ross 1971). Values thus act to guide buying behavior in such a way as to keep the elements of the concept consistent with one another.

An individual's value structure in Rokeach's paradigm can be viewed as comprised of two distinct value dimensions; terminal values and instrumental values. Terminal values are defined as the value of being or desired end states. Instrumental values are the values of doing and are aimed at reaching desired goals or end states. His paradigm can help us understand the role of values in shaping consumer perceptions of value in products. He lists 18 terminal and instrumental values which have been developed systematically based on rigorous research. The paradigm is regarded as generally

135

applicable for research in the United States, but the question remains open as to whether these values have strong generalizability elsewhere.

In spite of the rigorous testing and evaluation of Rokeach's framework, most researchers still have not sought to explore its full dimensions in a product purchase context. Such research is clearly needed. As observed by Arnold Mitchell of SRI International:

> In a marketplace of such staggering diversity the businessman would do well to emphasize the universal values. These are values which skewer the hierarchies vertically so to speak. Examples are comfort, nostalgia, beauty, fun, closeness, safety, naturalism, or escape. Any one of these is powerful enough to support an entire product line—indeed a whole industry (Mitchell 1980).

Rokeach's statements, however, provide only the rudiments of a framework for analyzing the influence of values on consumer perceptions of product value. John Howard thus has extended the work of Rokeach by modeling the specific relationships in a consumption context between self-concept, terminal values, and instrumental values. Rokeach had left the relationship between terminal and instrumental values largely unspecified, and also did not relate these values to consumer perception of value in products.

Howard regards terminal values as serving the evaluative dimensions of the self-concept (Howard 1977). Values, according to Howard, are used at all levels of the consumer decision process to determine the saliency of various choice criteria. Much of consumer behavior literature of course tells us that consumer attitudes toward a brand are based on choice criteria and that attitudes about these choice criteria lead to intention to purchase. Thus, the concept that individual beliefs influence attitudes is an underlying assumption of multi-attribute models.

Howard modeled the influence of terminal and instrumental values on product purchases in the context of extensive problem solving (EPS). EPS occurs when a consumer is faced with a decision on a brand in a product class with which the person is not familiar. The introduction of instant coffee to the market in the early 1940s is an example. Such decisions about a new product class take a long time and require the consumer to develop a new set of criteria by which to judge a product class and to determine the consistency of the product class with their value structure. Limited problem

solving (LPS) in contrast is a simpler decision because a
consumer only has to form decision criteria at this stage by
which to judge, for example, a new brand of coffee in the
product class of instant coffee. They need less information
and can make a decision more quickly. Finally, routinized
response behavior (RRB) occurs when consumers are familiar
with most of the brands in a product class and in essence
become brand loyal. Behavior then becomes habitual and largely unthinking.

Howard views consumer choice at the EPS stage as being
influenced by both terminal and instrumental values and as
operating at the level of both product class and brand. In
essence, terminal values guide decisions on the choice between
product classes i.e., the choice between regular and instant
coffee, and instrumental values guide choices of brands within
a product category, i.e., choice between several brands of
instant coffee. Instant coffee enjoyed slow acceptance in its
early years, for example, because it conflicted with the
housewives' terminal values of family security (taking care of
loved ones) and social recognition (respect, admiration).
Women serving their families instant coffee were perceived as
not caring for their families and hence were not as admired
as women preparing regular coffee (Haire 1950).

Figure 1 as developed by Howard further extends EPS to
show the process by which a given purchase might occur. The
model assumes that the consumer has made a choice about a
product class consistent with his/her terminal values. The
consumer is then guided in the purchase of a particular brand
by several instrumental values, in this case one of which
might be that of being logical (Step 1). Being logical could
be accomplished through several choice criteria, one of which
would be making a purchase on the basis of price (Step 2).

FIGURE 1
EXTENSIVE PROBLEM SOLVING ELABORATED

	(1) Instrumental values	(2) Choice criteria	(3) Salience	(4) Beliefs	(5) Contributions to attitude
Elements of the means-end chain	Logical	Price			
				Attitude	

Source: John Howard, Consumer Behavior: Application of
Theory (New York: McGraw Hill, 1977), p. 94.

137

Salience (Step 3) depicts the relative importance of various choice criteria such as price in support of the instrumental value of being logical. Step 4 is the consumers' belief about where a new brand lies on a given criterion, in this case whether price is high or low. One can then multiply salience by belief to get an operational measure of attitude toward a brand (Step 5). The contributions of all choice criteria are then summed for an overall measure of attitude toward a brand by the consumer. Thus, in summary, choice criteria for brand selection are based upon concept formation, and values, at least in the context of this model, are the source of choice criteria. A change in the saliency of choice criteria can of course take place in choosing a familiar brand in a product class. Also, changes in either the buyer's environment or values can occur which will influence brand selection.

We observed earlier that concept formation occurs at two levels, namely a choice between product classes and a choice between brands of a product. A choice between product classes would be, for example, a choice between regular and diet cola when colas are viewed as a product class. The second level of choice would be between brands within a given product class. Howard hypothesized that the lowest relatively stable level in a consumers' value structure is instrumental values. Instrumental values thus generate choice criteria at the level of a brand, and terminal values, operating at a higher level in the consumer's value structure, generate criteria for choosing among product classes. These hypothesized relationships were tested in a dissertation at Columbia University (Boote 1975). The two hypotheses were confirmed, namely that terminal values are not related to the level of brand choice but that instrumental values are related to brand choice. Specifically, terminal values appear to determine choice among product classes, while instrumental values determine choice among brands. Additional research is needed to further validate these findings but they appear soundly grounded in theory.

Finally, some fascinating research also is ongoing in industry today which seeks to further highlight the influence of values on consumer perceptions of product value. SRI, formerly the Stanford Research Institute, now is in the middle of a three year $1.3 million program called VALS (Values and Life Styles) (Marketing News 1979). The research is supported by more than 60 companies. Arnold Mitchell, the senior social economist for the project, and a person with a long history of study about the influence of values on product perception (Mitchell 1966; Mitchell 1971), contends that what people place high value on is the way in which things will go and that an understanding of values is vitally necessary for long range planning.

In 1978 the SRI surveyed business leaders who indicated
no less than 17 areas in which they felt information about
values would be important. Indeed, the SRI survey found that
46% of marketing researchers were using information on consumer values in their analyses. Overall, 82% of the marketers
said they should use such information. SRI research has
divided consumers for purposes of their analysis into three
broad categories: need driven, outer-directed, and inner-
directed. Their paradigm closely resembles the seminal work
of David Riesman in The Lonely Crowd which distinguished
between inner-directed and outer-directed people. The SRI
findings show that outer-directed consumers, the backbone of
the marketplace, buy with an eye to appearance--what other
people will think. Mitchell also found that a group he calls
the societally conscious, for example, stress simplicity,
frugality, conservation, and ecological soundness in product
selection and lean toward items made via so called "appropriate technology."

Many companies are supporting the VALS program, including
Polaroid, Mercedes Benz, Levi Strauss and others, all of whom
reportedly have found the values information useful in real
world situations. Mitchell points out, for example, that
Associated Merchandising Corporation identifies their customers
in terms of values in addition to standard demographics.
Similar marketing strategies, according to Mitchell, have been
developed by General Foods, J. C. Penney and others, and have
been employed in research on such activities as fast food
franchises, movie goers, credit cards, and musical instruments.
The framework for the VALS analysis was initially formulated
by utilizing the insights of the developmental psychologist
Abraham Maslow. Mitchell points out that "five of the nine
groups identified in the VALS research closely resembles
Maslow's hierarchy of human needs."

THE FUTURE OF VALUES RESEARCH

The question still remains somewhat unexplored as to
whether stable internal characteristics of consumers (i.e.
values) can be assessed in such a way as to be useful in
predicting purchasing behavior. Some of the studies previously discussed indicate that this can be done. The SRI research
also demonstrates that industry is actively involved in
supporting values research. Barry and Wooten feel that
consumers' values are an essential part in guiding the use of
future technologies insofar as they relate to the production
of consumable goods and services (Barry & Wooten 1973). They

present a different approach to the measurement of values than
the type of value inventories used in the '60s and '70s by
market researchers. They term this approach the "Consumer
Delphi" which is a systematic approach to assembling the
opinions of knowledgeable people as a means for gathering more
values information about potential consumers.

Strategically, values theory suggests that it may be more
productive to segment consumers on the basis of instrumental
values as opposed to various decision criteria reflective of
these values. Beliefs at the brand level can change quite
quickly. For example, prices over time become one way for
consumers to identify products. Price changes, however, may
cause consumers rather quickly to view a product in an entirely different light or even in a new product class.

Although values are fundamentally stable, they are not
rigid; they do bend with the environmental stresses of the
times. For example, the SRI research predicts that in the
'80s there will be a greater demand for the authentic and
natural. This means less emphasis on plastics and more emphasis on wood, wool, and cotton; also fewer replicas and more
originals, handmades, imports, and antiques. Also predicted
is a shift in emphasis from quantity toward quality and
simplicity. Management in the '80s would thus do well to
emphasize the universal values of comfort, nostalgia, beauty,
fun, closeness, safety, naturalism or escape (Mitchell 1980).

Similarly, promotional strategies which appeal to
centrally held values may be the most effective. Such efforts
would not only point out the attributes and the choice
criteria relative to a product, but would also reinforce
instrumental values associated with the product. As observed,
"a department store, for example, knowing that consumers in
their target market held the consumption values 'care about
the needs of individual consumers' and 'prompt service on
complaints,' and that these were in turn connected to the
global values polite and cheerful, might initiate an advertising campaign emphasizing courteous, helpful personnel and
the store as a pleasant cheerful place to shop" (Vinson,
Scott & Lamont 1977). Additionally, knowing the preferences of
large market segments will allow promotional efforts to be
better tailored in the choice of media.

Explicit emphasis on the enduring influence of relatively
stable value structures will require management to place
greater emphasis on market planning and will require a longer
planning horizon. More explicit emphasis on strategy is
needed. For example, a focus on anticipated markets by
evaluating consumers' current brand concepts is useless

because they change too rapidly for use as a base from which to plan.

We are not arguing that companies should abandon efforts to influence consumer choice criteria at the brand level since success in shifting these choice criteria is highly possible. However, these criteria, because they are subject to change and thus somewhat unstable, may not provide the best bases for longer term promotional strategies. We are predicting that the '80s will be a decade of renewed interest in self. Values are a natural and logical starting point for examination and understanding of self concept and its impact on the market-place. A variety of values inventories and beginning empirical studies exist but there is room for much more creative thinking in regard to this elusive yet fundamental dimension of consumers' wants and needs and product choices. Also, such a framework may provide the theoretical underpinnings so badly needed as a basis for further research in retailing on perceptions of product value. The absence of strong theoretical underpinnings has been one of the greatest weaknesses of much retailing research (Hirschman & Stampfl 1980).

REFERENCES

Barry, T. E. and Wooten, L. M. (1973), "Forecasting Consumer Values," European Journal of Marketing, 11.

Bither, Stewart W. and Miller, Stephen J. (1969), "A Cognitive Theory View of Brand Preference," in R. D. McDonald, ed., Marketing Involvement in Society and the Economy, Chicago: American Marketing Association, 280-286.

Boote, A. S. (1975), "An Exploratory Investigation of the Roles of Needs and Personal Values in the Theory of Buyer Behavior," Unpublished doctoral dissertation, Columbia University.

Brim, Orville, et al. (1962), Personality and Decision Processes, Stanford: Stanford University Press.

Darden, William (1980), "A Patronage Model of Consumer Behavior," in Ronald Stampfl and Elizabeth Hirschman, eds., Competitive Structure in Retail Markets: The Department Store Perspective, Chicago: American Marketing Association, 43-52.

Dolich, Ira (1969), "Congruent Relationships Between Self-Image and Product Brands," Journal of Marketing Research, 6 (February), 80-84.

Grubb, Edward L. and Grathwohl, H. L. (1967), "Consumer Self-Concept, Symbolism, and Market Behavior: A Theoretical Approach," Journal of Marketing, 31 (October), 22-26.

Gutman, Jonathan and Vinson, Donald E. (1979), "Value Structures and Consumer Behavior," in William Wilkie, (ed.) Advances in Consumer Research, Vol. 6, Chicago: American Marketing Association, 335-339.

Haire, Mason (1950), "Projective Techniques in Marketing Research," Journal of Marketing, 14 (April), 649-656.

Henry, Walter A. (1976), "Cultural Values Do Correlate with Consumer Behavior," Journal of Marketing Research, 13 (May), 121-127.

Hill, R. et al. (1970), Family Development in Three Generations, Schenkman.

Hirschman, Elizabeth and Ronald Stampfl (1980), "Retail Research: Problems, Potentials, and Priorities," in Ronald Stampfl and Elizabeth Hirschman, eds., Competitive Structure in Retail Markets: The Department Store Perspective, Chicago: American Marketing Association.

Howard, John (1977), Consumer Behavior: Application of Theory, New York: McGraw-Hill.

Lessig, V. Parker (1975), "A Measurement of Dependency Between Values and Other Levels of the Consumer's Belief Space," Journal of Business Research, 3 (July).

Marketing News (1979), "Information on Values and Lifestyles Needed to Identify Buying Patterns," (October 5), 1.

Mitchell, Arnold (1980), "Changing Values and Lifestyles," Paper presented at the 11th Annual American Marketing Association Attitude Research Conference, La Costa, California (March 4).

_____ (1971), "Changing Values and the Marketplace," in Fred C. Allvine, ed., Marketing in Motion-Relevance in Marketing, Chicago: American Marketing Association, 612-615.

Rokeach, Milton (1973), The Nature of Human Values, New York: The Free Press.

Ross, Ivan (1971), "Self-Concept and Brand Preference," Journal of Business, 44, 38-50.

142

Scott, Jerome E. and Lamont, Lawrence M. (1974), "Relating Consumer Values to Consumer Behavior: A Model and Method for Investigation," in Thomas Greer, ed., Combined Proceedings of the American Marketing Association, Chicago: American Marketing Association, 283-288.

Stampfl, Ronald W. (1978) "The Post-Industrial Consumer," Journal of Home Economics, January.

Stein, Karen and Stampfl, Ronald (1980), "Consumer Values: The Underpinnings of Consumer Values in a Post Industrial Society," paper presented at the Annual Meeting of the American Council on Consumer Interests, San Diego, Cal.

Vinson, Donald E. (1978), "Human Values and the Marketing Functions," in Richard Ericson (ed.) Avoiding Social Catastrophes and Maximizing Social Opportunities: The General Systems Challenge, Washington, D.C.: Society for General Systems Research, 298-305.

Vinson, Donald E. and Munson, J. Michael (1976), "Personal Values: An Approach to Market Segmentation," in Kenneth E. Bernhardt, ed., Marketing: 1776-1976 and Beyond, Chicago: American Marketing Association, 313-317.

Vinson, Donald and Nakanishi, Masao (1976), "Structural Composition of the Consumer Value-Attitudes System," Working paper series, Graduate School of Management, University of California, Los Angeles.

Vinson, Donald E., Munson, J. Michael, and Nakanishi, Masao (1977), "An Investigation of the Rokeach Value Survey for Consumer Research Applications," in William Perreault, ed., Advances in Consumer Research, Vol. 4. Chicago: Association for Consumer Research, 247-251.

Vinson, Donald, Scott, Jerome and Lamont, Lawrence (1977), "The Role of Personal Values in Marketing and Consumer Behavior," Journal of Marketing (April), 44-50.

White, Irving S. (1966), "The Perception of Value in Products," in Joseph W. Newman, ed., On Knowing the Consumer, New York: John Wiley and Sons, 90-106.

PRODUCT POSITIONING AND SEGMENTATION STRATEGY: ADAPTABLE TO RETAIL STORES?

Eleanor G. May, University of Virginia, Charlottesville

ABSTRACT

Product positioning and segmentation strategy has been used by retail researchers to assist managements in understanding their businesses. However, it appears that applications of these marketing concepts are limited in retailing by the nature of retailing itself - the fact that most retail establishments have locational constraints that limit both the size and the characteristics of the consumer segment to be served.

INTRODUCTION

Product positioning and segmentation strategy have been found to be extremely useful by marketers when analyzing marketing problems. But have these concepts become meaningful to retailers? Are there practical applications in retailing? And if meaningful and practical, how and where in retailing can product positioning and segmentation strategy be applied most effectively?

MARKET POSITIONING

What is product positioning and segmentation strategy? A definition presented recently by Professor Yoram Wind (1980) was:

> A product's positioning is the place a product occupies in a given market, as perceived by the relevant group of customers; that group of customers is known as the target segment of the market. Businessmen have been positioning their products to appeal to target segments since shortly after the serpent offered an apple and not an orange to Eve and not to Adam; however, they have not always done so consciously, or successfully. More recent experience shows that systematic analysis increases the success rate.
>
> Although such analysis has become quite sophisticated in recent years, there is still a tendency to analyze positioning and segmentation independently, largely because of the technical diffi-

culties involved in analyzing both simultaneously. In the last two or three years, however, a
number of decision-making models have been
developed for simultaneous analysis of positioning and segmentation.

This and other advances in positioning and segmentation research are clearly going to be a
boon for marketing and for the corporation as a
whole. Among several broader applications is an
attempt to integrate positioning and segmentation analysis with a company's overall strategic
planning. Should a company enter a new market?
Should it drop an old product?

Professor Wind extended his discussion of product positioning and market segmentation to the importance of developing a "product portfolio" and to extending the concept of positioning from individual products of a total corporation.
This latter he asserts is especially observable in retailing.
He gives as examples the "carriage trade" images of Saks
Fifth Avenue, Neiman Marcus, I. Magnin, and Dunhill and the
"entirely different image" of K mart. However, the vast
majority of consumer dollars expenditures for department-
store-type merchandise occur in a wide assortment of outlets occupying positions somewhere between these high price
and high fashion outlets and K mart and other discounters.
The important issue for consideration here is the challenge
of positioning and segmentation strategy to these Macy's,
Marshall Field's, Casual Corner, The Gap, Sears, Penneys,
and so forth.

EARLY RETAIL IMAGERY RESEARCH

It is safe to say that the first significant application
of the concepts of product positioning to retailing, even
though it was neither identified nor perceived as product
positioning, was image research. The idea that the image
concept could be applied to the retail scene was introduced
by Pierre Martineau (1958). He suggested the following
definition of store personality or image: "the way in which
the store is defined in the shopper's mind, partly by its
functional qualities and partly by an aura of psychological
attitudes."

The next phase in the development of retail imagery, major contributions to which were made by some of the people
at this conference, concentrated on the techniques of measuring images of retail outlets and tended to ignore the application of the research. Technique and/or technological

145

development is usually a necessary step in the development of a new process or system. But as a result the major immediate limitation of the early image efforts appears to be the minimal usage of the findings by retail store managements.

A number of factors are now apparent that help to explain the lack of acceptance of image research by retailers, not the least of which was the time and money involved. Most such studies cost at least $50,000, some were measurably over $100,000. We need to be reminded that most retailers have difficulty in conceiving of spending this amount on a project from which the expected return on investment might not be measurable and could possibly produce no return. Furthermore, whatever return there might be would be deferred until some indeterminable future date. Retailers typically on a daily basis make decisions of this size, in which similar amounts of money are spent to acquire merchandise or to acquire personnel or facilities to support the sale of this merchandise. But the dissimilarity between a research expenditure and other expenditures lies in the fact that the returns from the latter are predictable and usually they are relatively immediately available, or at least the timing of the payoff is predictable. Obviously, therefore, given a choice a retailer would almost always choose a non-research investment over a research investment and the research investment will be approved after nearly all non-research options have been elected.

Thus the major problems in management attitudes toward early image research were the small perceived usefulness and the high costs. In addition researchers were trying to meet the challenge of insufficient computer programs to properly handle the masses of data that could be and were being obtained in image research. Fortunately, the computer limitation has been overcome; and now the challenge to researchers is how to make useful the vast quantity of tabulations that can be produced.

Perhaps the lack of operational application of the findings from image research was a necessary and worthwhile phase in the development of positioning and segmentation research. The apparent limited usefulness served to force many researchers to restudy image research in order that ways be found for the results to be in such a form that the managerial applications would be more readily apparent. Or if this were not possible, the research and analysis needed to be altered in order that management could find that results as presented would fit the business's needs.

But as we take a second look at the early image research, it is evident that a major limitation was that the
status quo was being measured; that is image studies involved no longitudinal or serial data, and more importantly
they gave no indication of the potential future effect on
the business of a shift in the image, i.e., a repositioning
or a new segmentation strategy.

CURRENT IMAGE RESEARCH

Image research has now come into its own with the work
of such people as King, Ring, and Tigert (1980a and 1980b)
as well as in individual store studies (not described here
because of their proprietary nature). Apparently what has
made current image research practical, acceptable, useful,
is that the image findings have been applied to analysis of
store positionings.

Thus the in-depth image research of the 1960's and early
1970's paid off. But there must be other potential uses;
the opportunities from product positioning and market segmentation in retailing have not been exhausted by these recent
applications. Whether and how the existing limitations can
be handled are questions which lead to the core of the problems in trying to apply product positioning and segmentation
strategy to the retail milieu.

RETAIL POSITIONING VIS-A-VIS PRODUCT POSITIONING

For understanding of this point let's go back to Professor Wind's definition of product positioning and market segmentation: "the place a product occupies in a given market,
as perceived by the relevant group of customers; that group
of customers is known as the target segment of the market."
When one attempts to translate this definition into retail
terminology one immediately encounters problems. The first
one and the most important conceptually is difficult to explain but it encompasses the core of the difference between
retailing and marketing. That is a retail outlet's "place"
in a given market once selected is fixed. The geographic
place determines the demographics and psychographics of the
consumer segment of the retailer, in that the consumer segment to be served is limited by the type and number of customers residing in the trading area. A product's place in
the market, geographically, demographically, and/or psychographically, occasionally changes. Similarly, the place in
the market of a product can be broadened or it can be aban-

147

doned, with resulting positive impact on the overall profit
picture of the firm producing the product.

But a retailer is restricted in attracting customers by
his geographic position in the market; he is limited in his
ability to attract customers to patronize his store by the
density and size of the trading area, as well as the demographics and psychographics of the shoppers residing in the
trading area. A product, however, can be positioned to
serve a market segment with only limited consideration as to
whether the market is geographically disperse or geographically concentrated. The individual product and its consumers can and do interface in a multitude of institutional
types and geographic locations. But a retail firm has only
one or a limited number of locations in which to interface
its customers, in which to reach its market segment. It is
like a one-way street, but the arrow points in one direction
for the product and in the other direction for the retailer;
or in the extreme cases, the retailer may find a DO NOT
ENTER sign at both ends of the street.

BRANCH UNITS AS MEANS TO OVERCOME GEOGRAPHIC RESTRAINTS

Retailers have two options to overcome at least in part
these locational constraints on their operations. One is
the move to branch stores in the suburbs and to more distant
locations in other metropolitan areas. However, this type
action, taken by many retailers, may have compounded the
problem, rather than assisted in solving it. With additional locations, the retail firm still is locationally restricted in its positioning. The variety of locations may
result in need for a variety of positions, rather than
efficiencies being obtained because of similar consumer demographics and psychographics in the various locations.

CATALOG SELLING AS MEANS TO OVERCOME GEOGRAPHIC RESTRAINTS

Mail order or catalog selling has helped retailers to
solve the problem of interface with the specific consumer
segment for whom the retailer is positioned. Initially
catalogs were developed to reach the rural customers who
lived outside the trading area of most stores (McNair and
May 1976). Later the big catalogs (Sears, Wards, Aldens,
etc.) began to serve an additional function in the distribution institutional array; this new function of the catalog
was to supplement the merchandise available in the stores.
A major objective of most retailers involved in mail order

selling today is to have a medium to reach a geographically disperse consumer segment.

Many specialty mail-order catalog firms (e.g. L. L. Bean, Talbot's, Horchow's, Spencer) have developed as a result of a realization by managers of the business that their customer segments were too diffuse to be efficiently served from one or a few selling locations. With a catalog, the institution (the mail-order catalog) goes to the customer rather than the customer going to the fixed-location institution to acquire the desired products.

With the telecommunication shopping of the future, the advantages of mail order will be available to more consumers for more products and the geographic market restrictions of retail institutions will be overcome in large part.

SHIFTS IN RETAIL MARKET POSITIONS

But let's return for a moment to the Ring et al studies. They are worthy studies of market positioning of retailers, studies that retailers have found useful and they continue to serve as models for other research. Furthermore, they have been conducted over a span of years in a number of locations and as a result longitudinal data are available that serve to measure shifts in perceived positioning. These shifts may be the results of strategic positioning decisions or they may be caused by changes in the characteristics of the customers patronizing the stores.

The ability of a retailer to effect a substantial shift in the position of his store is severely restricted, restricted by the historically developed image of the firm, by the fixed physical location(s) of the firm, and by the characteristics of consumers in the market area. Only when a firm happens to be involved with a major shift in one of these dimensions can the firm experience a major shift in position.

The shift in position usually is the result rather than the cause. For instance, in a real life situation in a market in which the downtown stores continued to hold a significant share, a major retail component of the market moved into a completely new facility in a new downtown location. As a result the firm's position in the market was altered measurably, as judged by consumers and customers.

But most retailers are not in a situation in which it is practical, nor would it necessarily be effective, to build a new anchor store, Further,the addition of,or a conversion to, a broad-scale mail order operation is not feasible. Therefore, most shifts in retail positions are extemely minor and over a fairly long period of time. Even these shifts usually are the result of new competition in the market or other major changes in the marketplace, rather than being caused by specific action on the part of the retailer. Furthermore, the result of a market change may not be of sufficient size to be discernible in the retail positioning, as judged either by the consumers' perceptions or on the bottom line of the operating statement.

PORTFOLIO POSITIONING

Now let's return to Wind (1980) and further explore his comments about "incorporation of positioning and segmentation into a product/market portfolio." In applying this concept to positioning the corporation, he says: "Corporate positioning is the implicit focus of most public relations departments, but beyond that most corporations devote precious little time to the activity, either in terms of resources or in terms of attention by top managers." This statement may be true for many firms involved in marketing, but I believe that most retail companies are exceptions to Wind's generalizations. In retailing the store is the portfolio, that is, the portfolio is the complex of merchandise and service. And in retailing the "product" portfolio is the market position of the store; the store is the product.

Retail executives may not perceive themselves as being involved in corporate positioning or as developers of portfolios. But when one analyzes what retailing really is, it becomes apparent that virtually every action of all retail employees, not only those in public relations (in fact those in retail public relations may have only very limited impact), affect the firm's perceived market position. The day-to-day decisions in retailing are the bedrock of the definition and solidification of the firm's position in its market.

EXAMPLES OF RETAIL POSITIONING

Wind says, "Some companies, especially in the retail and service industries, are exceptions to the rule. Saks Fifth Avenue, Neiman Marcus, I. Magnin, and Dunhill all work hard at maintaining their images as purveyors to the carriage trade. The name K mart, on the other hand, conjures up an entirely different image, one that the company executives work equally hard to maintain in the minds of the American public." He adds a parenthetic remark: "one of the problems that Sears has had in the apparel area has been the lack of a clear identity as to the type, quality, and range of merchandise it offers."

One needs to understand completely that for most retailers, Sears included, the firm's market position is the result of externalities to the firm itself. Many retail positions, however, have developed by default rather than by analysis of the market to determine the segment whose needs or wants can best be served by the retailer. Product positioning typically involves the development of a position prior to product introduction (or reintroduction) rather than the post facto situation that occurs in retailing. Adaptations of market positions of existing retail firms, however, have been acomplished primarily as a result of changes in the markets themselves, mainly changes in the makeup of the consumers, as well as changes in economic conditions and in technology, not through efforts of the retailers themselves.

A number of examples can be identified in which retailers attempted to reposition their firm with the stated purpose that the firm serve a different consumer segment from that historically served. There are the experiences of the W. T. Grant Company, in particular when the firm began operating Grant City discount stores, also Peck & Peck, Bonwit Teller, A & P WEO, among others.

Of course, one can also name success stories involving repositioning of a retail store, the one probably most frequently cited is Bloomingdale's. But did Bloomingdale's repositioning involve a determination of a new market segment which it deemed feasible and profitable to be positioned for? Or rather did Bloomingdale's, perceiving that the market area characteristics of its main store were changing significantly, determine the wants and needs of the emerging consumer segment of this geographic area, a segment that would be of sufficient size to be profitable, and then the management developed the store to best serve the wants and needs of this new segment?

One retail historian (Hendrikson 1979) explained the Bloomingdale's phenomena as follows:

> Some competitors say that Bloomingdale's
> wouldn't succeed elsewhere, that it owes its

151

special cachet to what amounts to luck -
namely its unique location. Sour grapes,
replies Bloomies, and points to its thriving
branches in 15 other places. The Bloomingdale's customer does seem to represent a
state of mind rather than a geographic base,
but there is no denying that Bloomies is one
of the few, if not the only, department store
remaining [in 1976] whose flagship store does
business equal to the combined volume of its
branches.

When considering the Bloomies strategy, it should be
kept in mind that Bloomies merchandises its branches separately from the Lexington Avenue store; thus acknowledging
that its main store location is unique in both the consumer segment to be served and the best strategy (today it
would be called strategy, not luck) to satisfy these
customers.

And similarly there are the experiences of K mart and
Woolco. In these cases Kresge's and Woolworth's managements
perceived a growing consumer segment that was not being
served; for this consumer segment a new retail type was
developed and the concept was implemented. The consumers
were analyzed to determine their marketplace needs and new
business entities were developed. There was not simply a
shift in Kresge's or Woolworth's "portfolio."

Similar strategic developments in positioning and segmentation are apparent when one studies Dayton-Hudson's move into Target Stores and B. Dalton Bookstores; the growth of
specialty chains such as Radio Shack, The Limited, The Gap,
Brooks Fashions, Toys "R" Us, and so forth; and the introduction of such names as Bloomingdale's and Neiman Marcus
into geographic markets at some distance from headquarters
stores. These geographic moves presumably resulted from
indications of the existence of a large enough market
segment, demographically and psychographically, to support
the particular specialty of the firm in question; that is
there was a position in the market which the specific firm
had the special ability to serve.

Another retailing decision that implies a conscious attempt at repositioning a store unit to better satisfy the existing consumer segment is Carter Hawley Hale's change of
the name of the White Plains store from Bergdorf Goodman to
Neiman Marcus. Obviously there were some managerial considerations involved in this move, but certainly the perceived

market position of these names, and other Carter Hawley Hale names, must have been considered in this unusual step.

SHOPPING CENTER POSITIONING

The growth and development of regional shopping malls suggests that the challenge in retail positioning has become even more complex. Consumers are tending to make more patronage decisions based on the shopping complex instead of the individual store or the product. Thus the positioning issue has moved to a higher level, from product to store to shopping complex.

In a recent study (Prestwick 1980), 53% of the sampled shoppers in a major shopping mall reported they "definitely planned to visit a particular store or stores when they came to the center that day, and 60% of these stores were anchor stores." The other 47% of the respondents apparently came for the mall itself; the study did not report whether the attraction was mall activities, the social aspects of mall shopping, the complex of stores and services, or something else. The surprising finding, however, is that almost half did not make their shopping locational choice because of a specific store, but rather instead were attracted by some other aspect of the mall and its complex of units.

Another limitation in the effective application of product positioning and market segmentation in retailing is the virtual impossibility of a retailer to withdraw from the market successfully when the customer segment has become too small to support the "product," i.e, the store. It is not an uncommon procedure for a manufacturer with a portfolio of products to discontinue a product that has become unprofitable because the market segment the product serves has become too small to profitably distribute the product. Also the manufacturer frequently introduces a new product which will better serve the market.

But it is a virtual impossibility for a retailer to successfully replace all identifying signs and labels in and about the store, that is, change the image and the market position, and as a result be successful in attracting a new market segment. The investment in fixed assets, in inventory, and in goodwill developed over time is too large to simply write it off. Thus a retailer will tend to stick with his historic market segment, even when the segment appears to be weakening, in the hopes that the wheel will turn again and the market will revert to its previous characteristics.

CONCLUSION

In summary, the proponents of product positioning assume the product is the determinant of the purchase, but in retail positioning the determinant of patronage is the store. (Or is it the shopping complex?) And in product positioning and segmentation strategy the product variables primarily are image, except for location, a variable that generally is not feasible to alter once it is determined. The determination of retail position is a fairly well developed art. The question is whether retail repositioning is feasible except in most unusual situations.

REFERENCES

Hendrikson, Robert (1979), The Grand Emporiums, The Illustrated History of America's Great Department Stores. New York: Stein and Day.

King, Charles W., Lawrence J. Ring, and Douglas J. Tigert (1980a), "Fashion Involvement and Retail Shopping Behavior," Competitive Structure in Retail Markets: The Department Store Perspective, Ronald W. Stampfl and Elizabeth Hirschman, American Marketing Association, 88-97.

McNair, Malcolm P. and Eleanor G. May (1976), The Evolution of Retail Institutions in the United States, Marketing Science Institute, (April).

Martineau, Pierre (1958), "The Personality of the Retail Store," Harvard Business Review, 36 (January-February), 47-55.

Prestwick, Leonard (1980), "The Competitive Position of a Small Local Shopping Center," presentation to American Collegiate Retail Association, (April 12).

Ring, Lawrence J, Charles W. King, and Douglas J. Tigert (1980), "Market Structure and Retail Position," Competitive Structure in Retail Markets: The Department Store Perspective, Ronald W. Stampfl and Elizabeth Hirschman, American Marketing Association, 149-160.

Wind, Yoram (1980), "Going to Market: New Twists for Some Old Tricks," The Wharton Magazine, (Trustees of the University of Pennsylvania), 4 (Spring), 34-39.

THE DECISION TO USE PRODUCT INFORMATION
AT THE POINT OF PURCHASE[1]

J. Edward Russo, University of Chicago

ABSTRACT

Consumers decide whether to use product information by comparing the costs of information processing with the expected benefits in a modified cost/benefit analysis. The total processing cost is partitioned into three components: information collection, comprehension and computation. A similar cost/benefit analysis is performed by information providers, with consumer use an important benefit.1

PRODUCT INFORMATION

We consider all product information that is posted for reading somewhere in the point-of-purchase environment. In most buying situations purchasers confront a surprisingly large amount and variety of such information. Manufacturers provide descriptive brochures, nutrition labels and Underwriters Laboratories' seal of approval; retailers provide signs denoting items on sale; and government requires the clear posting of prices and sizes, fiber identifications of fabrics and the grading of meat, fruits and vegetables. In any purchase environment, shoppers must cull the most useful product information from the surrounding profusion competing for their attention. This paper addresses the question of how these shoppers decide what information to use and what to ignore.

---

[1]This research was partially supported by Grant DAR 76-81806 from the National Science Foundation.

THEORY

Cost/Benefit Analysis

Consumers' decisions about whether to use particular product information are based on cost/benefit analysis. This analysis need not be formal or extensive. It may often be done quickly and crudely. For example, in a recent study of nutrition information posted in supermarket aisles, I videotaped shoppers. Of those who noticed the information, half glanced for no more than 1 second. Their decision not to process any longer had to be based on only the most approximate of cost/benefit evaluations. The analysis may also be based on stereotyped perceptions of benefits or costs, such as the presumption "They all have the same price," or on insensitive decision rules, such as "I buy whatever is on sale." The only requisite is that somehow shoppers decide whether the expected benefits of processing the information are worth the expected costs. We turn now to an investigation of the types of costs and benefits that shoppers encounter.

INFORMATION PROCESSING COSTS

We shall focus more closely on information processing costs than on benefits. Costs are more unavoidable, more amenable to analysis, and have received too little attention in the current literature (e.g., Ratchford 1980). Information processing costs fall into three categories: collection, comprehension and computation.

Collection Costs

The first component of the total information processing cost is the cost of collection, i.e. of physically gathering the information. For instance, it takes time and effort to read the nutrition labels of competing food products. Shoppers must walk down the aisle, reach for packages, and turn them to read the nutrition label.

Retailers recognize their customers' collection costs when they organize products by category not by manufacturer. Shoppers would shun a small appliance vendor who made them go to the Sunbeam section to find a Sunbeam fry pan and the General Electric section to look at the comparable GE fry pan. Grouping different brands of the same appliance reduces the cost of physically collecting the product information necessary for interbrand comparison.

Can collection costs be reduced? Are current store arrangements optimal or can retailers provide an additional service to their customers by reducing information collection costs? In a study of unit pricing, a single list that collected all unit prices lowered this processing cost and significantly increased the use of unit price information (Russo 1977). Figure 1 shows an example of this type of display.

FIGURE 1
SAMPLE OF UNIT PRICE LISTS

Fruit Cocktail	Size (oz.)	Total Price	Unit Price Price per Pound
Raggedy Ann	30	$ .97	$ .52
Cert. Red Label	29	.95	.52
Del Monte	30	1.05	.56
Generic	16	.59	.59
Raggedy Ann	16	.67	.67
Del Monte	17	.75	.71
Libby's	14	.75	.71
Del Monte	16	.75	.75
S & W	17	.81	.76
Raggedy Ann	8	.41	.82
S & W	16	.99	.99
Del Monte	8.75	.59	1.07
S & W	8.75	.75	1.36

Using the same listing concept, appliance retailers might gather the main attributes of information for a particular product category onto a single list. For example, the list could contain the following information for all brands: price, wattage, Underwriters' Laboratory approval, number of speeds or dial settings, list of "features", etc. Some aspects of the information, such as the physical style or design, can only be perceived by a visual examination of the appliance itself. However, many other attributes, including most of the important ones, could probably be gathered together on a single list, greatly reducing collection costs. In a pilot study, Lyle Hubbard and I have presented just such lists to shoppers and received favorable responses from them.

Comprehension Costs

The second processing cost, comprehension, refers to the effort required to understand and evaluate the information

157

collected. For example, most participants in this conference probably do not fully understand such product attributes as the chemical preservatives in food, the energy efficiency ratings of appliances, or the distortion levels of audio speakers. Our ability to comprehend these attributes is confined largely to their direction, i.e., whether more or less is better. It is harder to evaluate a certain amount more energy efficiency or less audio distortion.

In general, comprehension costs increase as knowledge decreases. In the extreme when knowledge is completely insufficient, comprehension cost can become an absolute barrier. This is the major reason for the paradox of lowest information use by those who need it most. Poorer, less educated shoppers generally use (point-of-purchase) product information least, even though their benefits are greatest (relative to income).

Can comprehension costs be reduced? There are ways that information providers can reduce the cost of comprehension. In the nutrition study referred to above, a summary rating of overall nutrition was used. An abbreviated version of the actual in-store display is shown in Figure 2. (Note that to lower collection costs a list format was also used.) To lower comprehension costs further the summary rating, called the "Nutrition Quotient", was grouped into only a few categories and described pictorially by stars. Thus, to judge which frozen vegetables was more nutritious, shoppers had only to count the stars. As it turned out, they ignored even this highly simplified display for reasons explained shortly. The interested reader may find it instructive to guess the cause of this disuse.

Computation Costs

The third and last type of information processing cost is computation. If comprehension is the understanding and evaluation of the individual components of information, computation is the combining of these individual components to make product comparisons. Examples are making price comparisons, which are computations within a single attribute or, more commonly, making trade-offs between various attributes, such as deciding whether to pay $X more to get Y units less distortion in an audio speaker. Computation costs also include the effects of memory limitations as, for example, when one cannot keep track of the prices of all brands. Several authors have recently addressed these costs, especially Johnson (1980) and Shugan (1980).

Can computation costs be reduced? Computational costs vary widely across different types of product information and

FIGURE 2
SUMMARY FORMAT OF PARTIAL LIST OF FROZEN VEGETABLES

NUTRITION [2]   FROZEN VEGETABLES
QUOTIENT   Serving Size   3.3 oz.

****	32.2	Spinach, Leaf, Birds Eye
****	12.4	Broccoli Spears, Birds Eye
****	10.4	Cauliflower, Birds Eye
***	6.5	Spinach, Leaf, Green Giant
***	5.0	Broccoli Spears, Green Giant
**	3.8	Mixed, Green Giant
**	3.6	Broccoli in Cheese Sauce, Green Giant
**	3.2	Mixed, in Butter Sauce, Green Giant
**	2.7	Peas, Sweet, Green Giant
**	2.2	Cauliflower with Cheese, Birds Eye
**	2.2	Spinach, Creamed, Green Giant
**	2.0	Peas, Leseur Baby, Green Giant
*	1.7	Broccoli, Bake & Serve, Green Giant
*	1.5	Cauliflower, Bake & Serve, Green Giant
*	1.2	Corn, Cut, Birds Eye
*	1.2	Spinach, Bake & Serve, Green Giant
*	1.0	Corn, Niblets, Green Giant
	.9	Potatoes, O'Brien, Ore-Ida
	.6	Corn, Niblet Cream, Green Giant
	.5	Potato, Golden Fried, Ore-Ida
	.4	Onion Rings, Mrs. Paul's
	.3	Potato, Pixie Crinkles, Ore-Ida

different   formats   for   presentation.   Comparing   prices   is

---

[2]The Nutrition Quotient measures the average nutritional
return per calorie. It is the average % U.S. RDA of the eight
leader nutrients (see Figure 3) divided by the percentage of
the daily allotment of calories (out of 2300) provided by the
food. A NQ of 1 indicates a nutritional return equal to the
calories consumed. NQ's above 1 mean more nutrition per
calorie; NQ's below 1 mean less. One star is awarded if the NQ
exceeds 1, 2 stars if it exceeds 2, 3 stars if above 4, and 4
stars if above 10.

usually relatively simple, because price is a single attribute. But how does one compare different frozen vegetables on the basis of overall nutritional value, or even just on the basis of the seven vitamins and minerals required on nutrition labels? Figure 3 depicts this information, 9 nutrition attributes for each of 22 frozen vegetables.

FIGURE 3
MATRIX FORMAT OF PARTIAL LIST OF FROZEN VEGETABLES

	C A L O R I E S	P R O T E I N	V I T A M I N A	V I T A M I N C	T H I A M I N E	R I B O F L A V I N	N I A C I N	C A L C I U M	I R O N
FROZEN VEGETABLES Serving Size 3.3 oz.									
Spin., Leaf, Birds Eye	20	4	160	30	6	8	*	10	6
Broc. Spears, Bds Eye	25	4	20	70	4	4	2	2	2
Cauliflower, Birds Eye	25	2	*	80	4	2	2	*	*
Spinach, Leaf, Grn Gnt	118	10	130	80	2	10	2	20	15
Broc. Spears, Grn Gnt	118	6	40	130	6	10	2	8	6
Mixed, Green Giant	59	4	50	10	4	2	2	2	4
Broc./Cheese, Grn Gnt	171	15	80	50	6	15	2	40	6
Mixed/Butter, Grn Gnt	171	8	130	25	8	6	6	2	8
Peas, Sweet, Grn Gnt	66	6	6	25	6	4	6	2	6
Caul./Cheese, Brds Eye	110	4	20	45	2	6	*	6	*
Spin./Crmd, Grn Gnt	250	15	70	40	6	15	2	25	15
Peas, Leseur, Grn Gnt	198	15	25	60	15	2	8	6	8
Broc., Bake, Grn Gnt	107	4	6	35	2	6	*	8	2
Caul., Bake, Grn Gnt	90	4	4	25	2	4	*	6	2
Corn, Cut, Birds Eye	70	4	4	10	4	2	6	*	*
Spinach, Bake, Grn Gnt	123	6	10	6	4	10	*	10	4
Corn, Niblets, Grn Gnt	85	4	4	10	2	2	6	*	2
Pot., O'Brien, Ore-Ida	66	2	*	10	2	*	4	*	2
Corn, Cream, Grn Gnt	237	8	2	20	6	6	8	*	2
Potato, Fried, Ore-Ida	143	4	*	10	4	*	6	*	2
Onion Rngs, Mrs Paul's	198	6	*	*	4	4	10	*	2
Pot., Pixie, Ore-Ida	187	2	*	8	4	*	6	*	2

* denotes less than 2%.

Combining these individual nutrients into an overall measure of nutrition involves great computational effort. Consumers can be expected to ease this computational burden via simplifying assumptions and heuristics. The most common of these is ignoring many of the less important attributes. Of course, the price for this reduction in computation costs is an increasing chance of decision errors (Russo and Dosher 1980). Alternatively, the computation can be circumvented by presenting a summary rating of nutrition, as shown in Figure 2. A comparative inspection of Figures 2 and 3 makes clear the tremendous computational saving for any shopper who seriously wants to compare frozen vegetables on the basis of nutrition (and who accepts the Nutrition Quotient as a valid summary).

Just as the number of attributes of product information affects the cost of computation, so does the presentation format. For computational purposes, numerical formats are best. Pictorial and verbal representations are harder to enter into computations. For example, a pictorial format like a bar graph requires the extra computation of estimating the numerical magnitude from the pictorial representation. Imagine shoppers' difficulty in comparing prices if they were all presented as bar graphs.

BENEFITS

Benefits are much harder to classify than costs. Basically, the expected benefits are the value or utility of the particular information as perceived by shoppers. If chemical additives are considered an important component of food, then the perceived value of a listing of such additives will be high. In contrast, if the % U.S. RDA of riboflavin is almost never considered in food selection, then the value of this information will be practically zero.

Benefits are measured separately for each attribute of information and are highly subjective. Different people can have different utilities for the same product attributes. For some consumers cholesterol is an important dietary factor while others, because they have no health problems related to this component of food, derive little benefit from such information.

The problem for information providers is to estimate the average benefit of an attribute of information over the entire range of shoppers. Sometimes information is valued by all shoppers, as are prices and sizes. However, information to a particular market segment, such as those on low cholesterol diets, may still have a high enough utility to justify information provision.

161

The virtual absence of perceived benefits accounts for the failure of the nutrition information shown in Figures 2 and 3 to shift shoppers' purchases toward more nutritious foods. As best as can be determined, most shoppers are not concerned about the eight leader nutrients. In contrast, there is much broader concern about "negative nutrients", like sugar, salt, cholesterol and chemical additives. Thus, although the information format of Figure 2 reduces collection, comprehension and computation costs to a minimum, the total processing cost was not reduced below the low level of perceived benefits.

This example illustrates the flexibility of processing costs relative to benefits. Information providers will find it much easier to reduce costs than to increase benefits. The perceived benefit level serves as a target, beneath which costs must be reduced if shoppers are to use the presented information.

If this analysis is correct, what is the implication for the presentation of nutrition information at the point of purchase? We believe that unless the perceived benefits of the eight leader nutrients increase, the costs of processing this information (even when minimized as in Figure 2) will exceed the benefits. This does not imply, however, that other health-related information would not be used by shoppers. Given the greater concern with "negative" nutrients like calories, sugar and chemical additives, the perceived benefits of this information might well exceed the processing costs for a significant market segment. Figure 4 shows one such information display.

Changes in Benefits Over Time

Consumers base their decision to use product information on the benefits and costs that are momentarily apparent at the point of purchase. Although changes over time cannot alter processing costs, with the exception of comprehension costs, they can greatly alter perceived benefits. Historical trends in attitudes, experience with the product information, and use of the product itself can change perceived benefits. For example, the utility many people place on the health and nutrition aspects of food has increased considerably in the last ten years. Information that may have been ignored ten years ago, based on a cost/benefit analysis, might be consistently used today. Also, the benefits associated with product information are often not apparent until there has been a trial usage of that information.

162

FIGURE 4
CALORIE LIST OF SELECTED FROZEN VEGETABLES

FROZEN VEGETABLES Serving Size 3.3 oz.	CALO- RIES
Spinach, Leaf, Birds Eye	20
Broc. Spears, Birds Eye	25
Cauliflower, Birds Eye	25
Mixed, Green Giant	59
Peas, Sweet, Green Giant	66
Pot., O'Brien, Ore-Ida	66
Corn, Cut, Birds Eye	70
Corn, Niblets, Grn Gnt	85
Caul., Bake, Grn Gnt	90
Broc., Bake, Grn Gnt	107
Caul./Cheese, Birds Eye	110
Broc. Spears, Grn Gnt	118
Spinach, Leaf, Grn Gnt	118
Spinach, Bake, Grn Gnt	123
Potato, Fried, Ore-Ida	143
Broc. in Cheese, Grn Gnt	171
Mixed/Butter, Grn Gnt	171
Pot., Pixie, Ore-Ida	187
Onion Rings, Mrs. Paul's	198
Peas, Leseur, Grn Gnt	198
Corn, Cream, Green Giant	237
Spin., Creamed, Grn Gnt	250

Credibility

One last aspect of perceived benefits is credibility. This is viewed as a multiplicative factor attenuating the utility of the product information. For certain kinds of information such as unit pricing, credibility is high. Both shoppers' ability to verify the accuracy of unit prices in the store and laws prohibiting false price posting assure the credibility of such information. In contrast, credibility is low for the opinions of sales people, who are often thought to be biased by a competing self-interest.

163

THE COST/BENEFIT ANALYSIS OF INFORMATION PROVIDERS

So far, we have assumed that information is free to consumers. That is, the only cost for use is the processing cost of collection, comprehension and computation. We have not asked whether people are willing to pay for product information, i.e., to compensate the providers of the information.[3]

Provider costs. The costs to information providers include printing, posting, and other display costs, promotional expenses and the staff time to gather, analyze, or update the information. In addition, there are costs that are more long-term and harder to quantify, such as potential legal entanglements initiated by manufacturers whose sales are hurt by the new information.[4] Although these legal entanglements are sometimes designed more to harass than to win court judgments, they often succeeded because of the burden of costs they impose on information providers.

Provider benefits. Unfortunately, the compensating benefits to information providers are often much harder to apprehend. They are harder to quantify, especially in dollar terms, and harder to perceive because they are more long-term. For example, several supermarkets, including the Giant chain in Washington DC, and Jewel Food Stores in Chicago experienced a considerable increase in market share during the 1970's in conjunction with their taking a pro-consumer position. This position was partially manifested by the voluntary provision of

---

[3] Compensation cost might be added to the earlier three processing costs. When retailers' costs exceed their benefits, shoppers must compensate them for the provision of information. Usually, this compensation cost is borne in the form of higher prices.

[4] Manufacturer hostility can be reduced by describing products generically, rather than by brand name. Thus, food products in Figure 4 could be identified only as "Spinach, Leaf" or "Spinach, Creamed". No mention need be made of Birds Eye or Green Giant. The caloric values could then be obtained from the U.S. Department of Agriculture rather than requesting them from manufacturers. This eliminates the reliance on an uncertain cooperation by manufacturers.

significant amounts of product information.

Although not generally appreciated, there are several sources of short-term, dollar benefits to information providers. For example, when unit pricing was made more effective through the use of the list format shown in Figure 1, a substantial shift toward private labels occurred (Russo 1977). Averaged, over six product categories, the proportion of sales of private labels jumped from 35% to 40% of the total market. Since profits from private labels tend to be greater than profits from national brands, the retailer experienced a direct dollar benefit.

In the pilot test of small appliance information mentioned earlier, several types of information were used. Based on consumers' ratings, these could be divided into two classes, those that were thought to be at least somewhat effective and those that were considered essentially worthless. Only two of the six types fell into the latter category, one of which was the control treatment of deliberately useless information. All 13 shoppers who received the four useful types completed a purchase. For the worthless information, the sale was completed for only 2 out of 5 potential purchasers. Obviously, the sample base in this pilot study is small, and these results must not be interpreted as conclusive. However, they are illustrative of a potential benefit to retailers. If consumers find product information useful, they will be more confident in their ability to make a satisfactory purchase decision. This confidence will be translated into a willingness to complete the purchase rather than to move on to some other store in hope of a better range of products or better prices. Thus, increases in the market share of private labels and the proportion of completed sales are two examples of short-term dollar benefits to retailers as information providers.

Just as shoppers decide whether to use product information, retailers (or government policymakers or manufacturers) decide whether to provide it. The rationale of both decisions is captured in Figure 5. Cells 1 and 4 present no conflict. In Cell 1 both shoppers and retailers benefit from information provision. This ideal is rarely attained, although the supermarket shelf tags used for unit prices and inventory control numbers probably qualify. Unit pricing was initially resisted by supermarket executives, but the necessary shelf tags were soon discovered to provide a useful inventory control tool. Most chains would probably retain the shelf tags that were prompted by unit pricing even if unit price information were banned.

Equally noncontroversial is Cell 4, the product information graveyard. The net benefits of product information

FIGURE 5
JOINT COST/BENEFIT ANALYSES
OF SHOPPERS AND RETAILERS

Retailer   Shopper

                 Benefit > Cost   Cost > Benefit

	Benefit > Cost	Cost > Benefit
Benefit > Cost	1. Shelf tags for unit pricing and inventory control. Unit price lists? Appliance lists?	3. Universal Product Code (without price marking)
Cost > Benefit	2. Unit price lists? Appliance lists?	4. Product Information Graveyard

are negative to both retailers and shoppers. The nutrition
list of Figure 3 is an example of this; and even the easiest to
use list, Figure 2, may have to be buried in this doubly
negative category.

In Cells 2 and 3, the interests of retailers and consumers
conflict. For example, the Universal Product Code with
check-out via scanning offers benefits to supermarkets. These
benefits are increased considerably if the price marking of
individual containers can be terminated. But this, in turn,
imposes a cost on shoppers, namely the loss of price-marked
containers. Thus, the UPC with cessation of price marking
falls into Cell 3. Similarly, unit price lists (Figure 1) and
a brand-attribute matrix for appliances probably fall in Cell
2. They are beneficial to shoppers, but the net benefit to
retailers may be negative. This latter conclusion depends on
the benefits derived from the increased market share of private
labels (unit price lists) and the proportion of shoppers who
are turned into buyers by the appliance matrix. If these
increased profits do not cover provision costs, the net effect
is negative for providers.

When there is a conflict, there may still be a positive
net benefit combined over both shoppers and retailers. For

166

example, the shopper savings enabled by unit price lists may far exceed the retailers' net cost (Russo 1977). In such cases, the price mechanism permits a transfer of benefits. Consumers might be willing to absorb a small price increase, enough to make retailers' net benefits positive, in return for posting the lists. A substantial savings would presumably still accrue to shoppers. Similarly, if the cost reduction from cessation of price marking were passed on to consumers, they might accept the absence of prices on all individual containers.

CONCLUSION

This paper has argued for a cost/benefit analysis of point-of-purchase information, or rather two such analyses from the different perspectives of information providers and information users. Since the extent of shoppers' use of product information is a major factor in benefits to providers, the latter should attempt to understand shoppers' decisions to use such information. Specifically, we urge information providers to perform a cost/benefit analysis of information usage <u>from the shoppers' perspective</u>. Do the perceived benefits exceed costs? Can any of the information processing costs be lowered to generate greater use? These are questions that should be answered in designing and deciding whether to implement any new program of information provision.

REFERENCES

Johnson, Michael D. (1980), "An Information Processing Analysis of Product Labels," in <u>Advances in Consumer Research</u>, Vol. 7, Jerry C. Olson, ed., Ann Arbor, MI: Association for Consumer Research.

Ratchford, Brian T. (1980), "The Value of Information for Selected Appliances, <u>Journal of Marketing Research</u> 101 (February), 14-25.

Russo, J. Edward (1977), "The Value of Unit Price Information, <u>Journal of Marketing Research</u> 14 (May), 193-201.

_____, and Barbara A. Dosher (1980), "The Role of Cognitive Effort in Selecting Strategies for Binary Choice," University of Chicago.

Shugan, Steven M. (1980), The Cost of Thinking, <u>Journal of Consumer Research</u>, in press.

RETAILING THEORY: PERSPECTIVES AND APPROACHES

Bert Rosenbloom, Drexel University
Leon G. Schiffman, Baruch College, CUNY

ABSTRACT

Retailing is a complex and mysterious subject that can be viewed from a variety of perspectives. The development of more retailing theory could make a strong contribution to a better understanding of retailing from these different perspectives.

While a general theory of retailing is unlikely to emerge, the prospects for middle-range theories that treat particular aspects of retailing associated with the various perspectives are believed to be quite good.

INTRODUCTION

Retailing is most commonly defined as the activities involved in the sale of goods to ultimate consumers (Duncan and Hollander 1977). Such a definition suggests a very simple and practical process consisting of merchants buying goods, placing them in stores, and then selling them to consumers. Why then would theory be needed to deal with such a simple subject?

The answer to this question is simple. Retailing is not a simple subject. Rather it can be, and often is a complex and mysterious subject that could be made less complex and less mysterious through more retailing theory. Even if we accept retailing as consisting of only the rudimentary activities of buying goods, placing them in a store, and selling them to consumers, the potential role for theory is immediately obvious. For example, as any retail buyer will attest, buying the right kinds of merchandise, from the right vendors, at the right prices, and at the right times is anything but simple. A theory of retail buying could help. As any retailer knows, there is more involved in presenting merchandise at retail than simply stacking it up at random on the selling floor. A theory of merchandise presentation could help. Finally, virtually all retailers will concur that merely having merchandise available in a store is no guarantee that consumers will come in and buy it. A theory of consumer store patronage behavior could help.

Thus, even if retailing is viewed as the "simple" process of buying, stocking, and selling goods to consumers, theory could make a substantial contribution. But retailing can also

168

be viewed from several other perspectives, and here too, theory could make a strong contribution.

In this paper, we present several additional perspectives for viewing retailing and discuss the role that various approaches to retailing theory could play in fostering improved understanding of retailing.

PERSPECTIVES FOR VIEWING RETAILING

There are at least four perspectives for viewing retailing: 1) retail management of the firm, 2) retailing as a basic economic activity in the macro-economy, 3) retailing as a subset of the distribution channel, and 4) retailing as a social institution in society.

Retail Management Perspective

Retailing viewed from the perspective of the management of the retail firm is by far the most common perspective used both by academics and practitioners. The overwhelming majority of retailing literature is written either explicity or implicity from this perspective. Virtually all retail practitioners automatically take this perspective as a matter of necessity because they are dealing with the management of the retail firm on a daily basis. The so-called "simple" view of retailing discussed in the introduction to this paper is also a retail management perspective.

Essentially, when the retail management perspective is taken, retailing is viewed as the process of managing the activities involved in transferring the ownership rights to goods to final consumers. Such activities in their most basic form usually include, buying, selling, storage, promotion, merchandise presentation, inventory control, pricing, and financing. These activities can be performed by a retailer (either store, or non-store) or by some other type of institution that engages in retailing such as a manufacturer, wholesaler or non-profit organization.

The basic role of theory, from the retail management perspective, would be to provide improved understanding of retail management activities as a basis for making better retail management decisions. If a theory could explain the dynamics of the buying process, for example, retail buyers would presumably be able to make more effective buying decisions. Theories of inventory control might help retail managers to optimize their inventory levels while a theory or theories of customer shopping behavior would be useful for planning selling strategies and so forth. A general theory of retailing management

169

would cover all the major activities involved in retail management and would explain the interrelationships among all of the activities.

Retailing in the Macro Economy
Another way of looking at retailing is as a major economic sector of the macro economy. Retailing comprises a very significant portion of GNP, and total employment, and therefore has a major impact on the overall shape and performance of the economy.

When retailing is viewed as a sector of the economy the emphasis of interested parties, particularly government planners and those industries directly affected by the retailing sector, is on changing patterns of retail structure and performance. Questions such as the following are the focus of investigation:

1. How will changing patterns of retail employment affect the economy?

2. How will the growth of large scale vs. small scale retailing institutions affect the long-term health of the economy?

3. Why has productivity in retailing tended to lag far behind productivity in other sectors of the economy?

4. Does the development and merger of giant retailing organizations create anti-trust violations?

5. What retail institutional types have strong prospects for rapid growth in the future, and which retailing institutions are likely to decline?

These and similar questions are extremely complex and difficult to answer. A theory (or theories) dealing with the role of retailing in the macro economy could be of great value if it helped to make the relationships among the variables affecting any of these questions more explicit. For example, what is the relationship between capital investment and labor productivity in retailing? Does the relationship differ from that in the manufacturing sector, and if so, how? A theory of retailing productivity might help to make these relationships clearer and would surely provide a basis for more fruitful research on these questions.

Retailing and the Distribution Channel
This third perspective is one of retailers being viewed as middlemen in channels of distribution. While retailers occasionally take this perspective of themselves, it is primarily

held by manufacturers and wholesalers. To the latter, retailers are viewed as channel members through whom they can distribute their products to consumers.

Given this perspective of retailing, the kinds of issues that arise from the manufacturer or wholesaler's point of view revolve around the role played by retailers in the inter-organizational marketing system comprising the marketing channel. Among the most salient retailing issues that arise in this context are:

1. Should retailers be used in the channel to distribute the manufacturer's or wholesaler's products?

2. What type of retailers should be used to distribute the manufacturer's or wholesaler's products?

3. How can retailers be persuaded to carry the manufacturer's or wholesaler's products?

4. How can retailers be motivated to do an effective job of selling the manufacturer's or wholesaler's products?

5. What can be done to promote cooperation and avoid conflict between the channel members at the manufacturer, wholesaler, and retailer levels?

A retailing theory or theories viewed from the perspective of the manufacturer or wholesaler using retailers in the channel of distribution would tend to focus on retailer behavior as it relates to these and similar issues. For example, a theory of marketing channel design would attempt to explain the behavior of retailers so as to offer insight into whether retailers should or should not be used in the manufacturer's or wholesaler's channels of distribution. A theory or theories of retailer buying behaviors could help manufacturers and wholesalers to develop better strategies for getting retailers to carry their products. A theory of inter-organizational channel management would help manufacturers and wholesalers to develop better programs for motivating retail channel members and would help to explain the dynamics of cooperation and conflict between manufacturers, wholesalers, and retailers in the inter-organizational setting of the marketing channel. A general theory of the retailer's role in the marketing channel would attempt to deal simultaneously with all of the issues cited above as well as other related issues.

Retailing as a Social Institution in Society
The fourth and final perspective of retailing is one of re-

tailing as a social institution in society. In this view, retailing is seen as a major social activity in society that is
not only influenced by the society but helps to shape the
social-cultural norms, tastes and behavior of the society within which it exists. From a societal perspective of retailing,
retailers are seen as participants in the socio-cultural fabric of society and may even serve as change agents who influence many of society's socio-cultural patterns. The growth
of major suburban shopping malls, for example, has had a profound effect on the lifestyles of millions of people in the
post World War II United States. They have played a major role
in creating the suburban culture that is so pervasive in the
U.S. Indeed, the suburban culture as we know it, whether for
good or bad, could not exist without the ubiquitous shopping
centers and malls.

Tastes in art, design, fashion, music, and many other aspects of culture are also influenced by retailers, who certainly serve as purveyors of the so-called popular culture
(Hirschman and Stampfl 1980).

Unfortunately, because so little theory exists on retailing from a socio-cultural perspective, little is known about
how retailing affects the socio-cultural patterns of society
and the degree of retailing's influence.

Thus, a theory or theories of the role of retailing in
society would address these fundamental questions. Such theory
would help to clarify the interdependences that exist between
retailing and other institutions in shaping the socio-cultural
patterns in society.

APPROACHES TO RETAILING THEORY

It would indeed be desirable to have one comprehensive
theory of retailing that would address retailing from all four
perspectives cited above. The development of such a grand
theory of retailing, however, while perhaps not impossible to
expect, is certainly remote. Indeed even the development of
separate general theories covering each of the four perspectives of retailing is probably outside the realm of reality
in the foreseeable future.

What is far more reasonable to pursue is the construction
of limited theories dealing with particular aspects or issues
associated with each of the perspectives of retailing. Such
limited or middle-range theories, while not offering the generalizability of a comprehensive theory, could nevertheless help
to explain the phenomena within the prescribed boundaries co-

vered by the theory. Thus, a theory of retail buying viewed from the retail management perspective (see earlier discussion) would not be applicable to other aspects or issues in retail management nor to the issues associated with the other perspectives of retailing. But, if it is good theory, it would provide powerful insight into the phenomena of retail buying in the context of retail management.

The prospects for constructing limited retailing theories are reasonably good. In fact, some groundbreaking attempts at retailing theory construction have already been made. While most of this work is implicit and tentative and would typically not qualify as theory in the strict sense of the term (Hunt 1976), it nevertheless provides a starting point for the development of more explicit and rigorous middle-range retailing theories.

This work can be grouped into five categories based on the approaches taken by its authors. These are:

1. Retail-Entrepreneurial Theory

2. Retail-Institutional Change Theory

3. Macro-Retailing Theory

4. Retail Operations Theory

5. Retail Shopping Behavior Theory

Retail Entrepreneurial Theory
This area of retailing theory attempts to explain the dynamics of retailing, especially the development of new retailing institutions, in terms of the particular traits and abilities of individuals.

While no explicit theoretical work has been done in this area, the rich descriptive literature that exists is rife with implicit theories. Take, for example, the many historical books written about retail entrepreneurs (e.g., Filene 1924, Gibbons 1926, Hower 1946, Emmet and Jench 1950). Some of these books concentrate on interesting personalities, such as the poor immigrant merchant who is able to realize the "American dream" and go from "rags to riches" (Birmingham 1967, Harris 1979). Most of these books imply many cause effect relationships between the development of major new forms of retailing institutions and the personalities, skills, and behaviors of retail entrepreneurs.

This literature could provide the basis for explicit and

formal retail entrepreneural theories. Perhaps the most fruitful approach to the construction of such theories would be
through the systematic analysis of this literature via content
analysis to cull out the many implied hypotheses that relate retailing dynamics to innovative individuals. Once this has been
done, these implied hypotheses could be made explicit and formal. They could then be tested by tracing the accomplishments
of present day retail entrepreneurs who have founded important
retail organizations.

Retail Institutional Change Theory

This approach to retailing theory deals with the dynamics
of retailing in terms of evolutionary processes that account
for changes in the structure of retailing.

This area of retailing theory has received more attention
than any of the other areas in the sense that more identifi-
able theoretical models have been constructed using this approach to retailing theory. The most well known of these theoretical models are: the "wheel of retailing," (McNair 1958)
"the retail accordian,"(Hollander 1966) "the retail life
cycle," (Davidson, Bates and Bass 1976) "the quest for differential advantage," (Alderson 1957) and "the natural selection
process" (Dreesman 1968).

What is needed now to advance these groundbreaking theoretical models of retail institutional change are more attempts to operationalize the constructs and hypotheses contained in these models, as well as empirical research to test the
conflicting explanations offered by the alternative theories.
The outcome of this effort might be a synthesized, middle-range
"contingency" theory that reveals the "boundaries of appro-
priateness" of the explanations expoused by each of the theories.

Macro-Retailing Theory

As an approach to retailing theory, macro retailing theory
addresses the subject through perspective one (Retailing in the
Macro Economy) and three (Retailing as a Social Institution).
Work in this area has dealt with macro issues on retailing's
role in the economy and society in general (Holton 1953,
Bucklin 1972). Thus, such issues as the following have been
examined:

1. What societal-level benefits are provided by alternative types of retail institutions?

2. Do alternative types of retail institutions provide different levels of consumer satisfaction or
   welfare?

3. How does the society (environment) within which retailing institutions operate influence the structure and dynamics of retailing?

4. What kinds of environmental factors affect the
productivity of the retailing system, and how?

While formal macro retailing theories have not yet emerged,
continued work in this area should stimulate interest in theory
development since theory will be needed to provide structure
and guidance for further research into macro-retailing.

Retail Operations Theory
    Most of the work in retail operations theory conforms to
perspective one (Retail Management Perspective) Hence, it is
concerned with the management of retail operations at the micro
level.

With the possible exception of retail location, this area
contains little explicit formal theory; but there is a wealth
of implicit theories, hypotheses, and heuristics in the relatively vast literature of this area. Even some of the basic
texts on retail management contain allusions to theory in such
areas as buying, merchandise planning, store layout and display, inventory control and other phases of retail operations
(Gist 1968, Duncan and Hollander 1977). While it is true that
much of this material would at best be relegated to the realm
of "folk theory" or "rules of thumb" when measured against the
requirements for theory in the strict sense, its value should
not be dismissed out of hand. The wealth of crude descriptive
models, rules of thumb, "principles", and conventional wisdom
contained in this literature provide theorists with a ready
made inventory of propositions about the management of various
phases of retail operations. This in turn offers a valuable
starting point for more formal theory construction on retail
operations.

Retail Shopping Behavior Theory
    This theory area deals with the consumer behavior dimen-
sions of retailing (or the retailing dimensions of consumer
behavior).

If measured in terms of sheer quantity of research reported in the various journals that include marketing, consumer behavior, and retailing topics, the amount of work addressing
the interfaces between consumer behavior and retailing has been
great. Unfortunately, this extensive body of theory and research has yet to be synthesized into general or even middle-
range theories of customer shopping behavior in the retail set-

ting. What exists presently are essentially some customer-seg-
mentation taxonomies (Stone 1954, Darden and Reynolds 1971,
Tauber 1972), and a small "glossary" of concepts relating consumer behavior and retailing such as impluse buying, in-home
shopping, outshopping, store patronage behavior and loyalty,
shopping motivation, store choice behavior, and store image.
While this material is useful, it hardly begins to reflect or
take advantage of the rich, joint consumer-behavior/retailing
literature.

However, the existence of this large body of preliminary
theoretical constructs, concepts, and empirical research relating consumer behavior to retailing offers excellent potential
for the construction of more formal and rigorous middle-range
theories dealing with the many interfaces between retailing
and consumer behavior.

COMBINING THE PERSPECTIVES AND APPROACHES
TO RETAILING THEORY

The relationships between the four perspectives and five
approaches for developing retailing theory can be visualized
by using a matrix such as that shown in Figure 1. The four
perspectives are listed across the top of the matrix
and the five approaches are listed vertically at the left. The
twenty cells produced show the possible interfaces between the
perspectives and approaches to retailing theory. The check
marks indicate what areas the authors believe will offer the
greatest potential for further work in theory development given
a particular perspective and approach. For example, we believe
that further work using the entrepreneural approach to retailing theory could make its greatest contribution to retailing
under perspectives one and four.

CONCLUSION

Retailing, while often viewed as a simple and practical
subject, is actually a very complex and in some ways mysterious
subject. This is especially the case when retailing is viewed
from other perspectives besides the most common one of management of the retail firm. These other perspectives are those
that view retailing as a basic economic activity in the macro
economy, a subset of the distribution channel, and a social
institution in society.

The development of retailing theory could prove to be highly useful for gaining a better understanding of the complexities
and mysteries of retailing.

Figure 1. Retailing Theory Perspectives and Approaches

Perspectives / Approaches	Retail Management (1)	Macro Retailing (2)	Retailing in Marketing Channel (3)	Retailing as a Social Institution (4)
Entrepreneural Theory				
Institutional Change Theory				
Macro Retailing Theory				
Retail Operations Theory				
Retail Shopping Behavior Theory				

A general theory of retailing that treats all phases of retailing from all four perspectives, though perhaps not impossible to expect, is highly unrealistic. Thus, retailing theory is likely to be of a limited or middle-range type that addresses specific issues or questions associated with the different perspectives of retailing. The prospects for such middle-range theories are good because a substantial body of literature exists which can provide a foundation for the construction of formal retailing theories.

REFERENCES

Alderson, Wroe (1957), Marketing Behavior and Executive Action, Homewood, Illinois: Richard D. Irwin.

Birmingham, Stephen (1967), Our Crowd, New York: Harper and Row.

Bucklin, Louis P. (1972), Competition and Evolution in the Distribution Trades, Englewood Cliffs, NJ: Prentice-Hall.

Darden, William and Fred D. Reynolds (1971), "Shopping Orientations and Product Usage Rates," Journal of Marketing Research 7 (November), 505-508.

Davidson, William R., Albert D. Bates and Stephen J. Bass (1976), "The Retail Life Cycle," Harvard Business Review 54 (November-December), 89-96.

Dreesman, A. C. R. (1968), "Patterns of Evolution in Retailing," Journal of Retailing 44 (Spring), 64-81.

Duncan, Delbert J. and Stanley C. Hollander (1977), Modern Retailing Basic Concepts and Practices, Ninth Edition, Homewood, Illinois: Richard D. Irwin.

Emmet, Boris and John E. Jench (1950), Catalogues and Counties, Chicago: University of Chicago Press.

Filene, Abraham L. with Burton Kline (1924), A Merchant's Horizon, Boston: Houghton-Mifflin.

Gibbons, Herbert A. (1926), John Wanamaker (Vol. 2), New York: Harper and Brothers.

Gist, Ronald R. (1968), Retailing Concepts and Decisions, New York: John Wiley and Sons.

Harris, Leon (1979), Merchant Princes, New York: Harper and Row.

Hirschman, Elizabeth C. and Ronald W. Stampfl (1980), "Roles of Retailing in the Diffusion of Popular Culture: Micro-perspectives," Journal of Retailing 56 (Spring), 16-36.

Hollander, Staley C. (1966), "Notes on the Retail Accordion," Journal of Retailing 42 (Summer), 29-40.

Holton, Richard H. (1953), "Marketing Structure and Economic Development," Quarterly Journal of Economics 67 (August), 344-61.

Hower, Ralph M. (1946), History of Macy's of New York, Cambridge, Mass: Harvard University Press.

Hunt, Shelby D. (1976), Marketing Theory, Columbus, Ohio: Grid Inc.

McNair, Malcom P. (1958), "Significant Trends and Developments in the Postwar Period," in Competitive Distribution in a Free High-Level Economy and Its Implications for the University, A. B. Smith ed. Pittsburg, PA: University of Pittsburg Press, 1-25.

Stone, Gregory P. (1954), "City and Urban Identification: Observations of the Social Psychology of City Life," American Journal of Sociology 60 (July), 36-45.

Tauber, Edward M. (1972), "Why Do People Shop?," Journal of Marketing 36 (October), 46-49.

A THEORY OF MERCHANDISE BUYING BEHAVIOR

Jagdish N. Sheth, University of Illinois

ABSTRACT

A retailer's merchandise buying behavior is a function of his merchandise requirements, supplier accessability, and choice calculus with which he selects the best supplier. However, the actual choice of a supplier may be other than the best supplier due to ad hoc situational factors such as business climate, business negotiations, company's financial position and market disturbance.

INTRODUCTION

Although there is considerable knowledge about how consumers and producers buy products and services (Engel, Blackwell & Kollat, 1978; Howard and Sheth, 1969; Ferber, 1977; Sheth, 1977; Webster and Wind, 1972), surprisingly, we know very little about how a retailer makes his merchandise selection and purchasing. The retailer is neither like a consumer nor like a producer even though he is an integral entity in the vertical flow of goods from the producer to the ultimate consumer. In other words, he is unique, and therefore, any theory of merchandise buying behavior which is designed should take into consideration the uniqueness of his buying behavior.

In one sense, the retailer is much more like a consumer than a producer: Merchandise items he buys are primarily finished products rather than raw materials, components or parts. Furthermore, he has more working capital requirements similar to the consumer households. For example, he needs very little by way of machinery and plant but needs a large assortment of products for inventory. Consequently, his purchasing planning cycle is relatively short term and highly volatile comparable to the households.

In another sense, however, a retailer is a business entity, often a big business entity, with the same set of corporate objectives, legal and financial constraints, and multiple stakeholders to whom he is accountable similar to a producer. Consequently, he is more likely to document his merchandise buying behavior and manage the process of buying similar to the producer.

Logically, we can safely assert that a retailer is more like a consumer in what he buys, and more like a producer in how he buys his merchandise. In other words, the content of merchandising buying behavior should be similar to household buying behavior and the process of merchandising buying behavior should be similar to industrial buying behavior.

Since we know something about household buying behavior, and about industrial buying behavior, it should be possible to integrate the appropriate pieces of knowledge from the two areas of research, and generate a theory of merchandise buying behavior which is both unique and still similar to other areas of buying behavior. This paper represents an attempt toward developing such a theory.

DESCRIPTION OF THEORY

The theory of merchandise buying behavior described in this paper is less behavioral and more at a microlevel in its orientation and specificity following the recent criticism of past theories and research in consumer behavior (Sheth, 1979). Accordingly, the theory does not purport to describe and explain how an individual manager in the retail organization buys the merchandise. Rather, the theory describes and explains the merchandise buying behavior of the retail organization. It is, therefore, more an organizational buying behavior theory rather than a consumer buying behavior theory. Accordingly, all personal attributes such as personality traits, demographics, life styles, learning, values and perceptions associated with modeling individual decision-making process are explicitly left out from the theory. Instead, the theory incorporates company demographics and psychographics in order to take into account interorganization differences in merchandise buying behavior.

The theory of merchandise buying behavior is summarized in Figure 1. It consists of the following constructs: Merchandise Requirements, Supplier Accessability, Choice Calculus, Ideal Supplier/Product Choice, and Actual Supplier/Product Choice. Each construct will be described in more detail in the following pages.

Merchandise Requirements
It refers to the merchandise buying motives and their associated purchase criteria. There are both functional and nonfunctional merchandising requirements. The functional requirements refer to those buying needs which are a direct reflection and representation of what the retailer's customers want in merchandise at his retail outlet. A successful retailer is presumably the one who can assess his customer's needs/wants

181

A THEORY OF MERCHANDISE BUYING BEHAVIOR

FIGURE 1

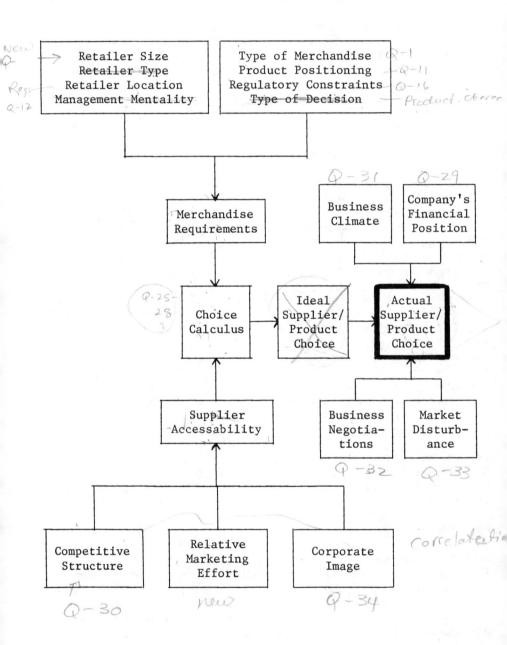

and properly translate them into his merchandise requirements.

The nonfunctional merchandising requirements reflect all other buying motives or purchase criteria including those based on imitating what competition does, personal values of the retail buyer, past traditions, reciprocity arrangements with suppliers or other non-market factors. Unfortunately, a significant number of merchandise buying decisions are driven by nonfunctional purchasing requirements resulting in losses for the company. This is particularly more true of smaller retailers as indicated by the vast number of business failures among small retail businesses.

The merchandise requirements will vary from one retail organization to another as a consequence of their own positioning and market niche decisions. The interorganizational differences in merchandise requirements are presumed to vary with such organizational characteristics as size (big vs. small) and type (discount vs. department store) of retail establishment, its location orientation (national, regional or local) and its management mentality (financially driven vs. merchandising driven company). These exogeneous factors can easily account for the differences among various retail establishments and, therefore, they are often used as market segmentation criteria by their suppliers.

The merchandise requirements will also vary from one product line to another within the same retail establishment. For example, a retail chain such as Sears will have different requirements between its automotive division and clothing division simply due to the nature of products involved. To account for these intraorganization differences in merchandise requirements, the theory postulates the following determinants: type of merchandise (dry goods vs. brown goods), product positioning (private label vs. national brand), type of merchandise decision (first time vs. repeat order) and legal/regulatory restrictions (FDA, USDA, FTC, antitrust, etc.). As would be expected, a specialty retail establishment will have few intraorganizational differences in merchandise requirements as compared to a shopping and a convenience goods retail establishment. Similarly, a small retailer will have less variations in his merchandise requirements than a big retailer partly because the former is likely to buy an assortment of products from a single jobber or wholesaler. Thus, with the emergence of superstores and supercatalogs, we should expect greater intraorganizational differences in merchandise requirements.

Merchandise requirements, therefore, represent retailer needs, motives and purchase criteria.

Supplier Accessability

It refers to the evoked set of choice options open to a
retailer to satisfy his merchandise requirements. Obviously,
not all suppliers are likely to be accessable to every retailer
except in the extreme and unlikely situation of perfect competition. On the other hand, the total number of suppliers for
retailers is likely to be considerably greater than those for
producers due to relatively lower barriers for entry and exit
experienced by distributors in general as compared to manufacturers. In fact, this may explain why there is a preference
for vertical integration in distribution or between manufacturing and distribution, since such arrangements tend to narrow
down the choice options available to other retailers and thus
reduce competition.

Three distinct but related factors are likely to account
for supplier accessability to a given retail establishment.
The first is the competitive structure of the supplier industry. For example, if it is a virtual monopoly, the choice of
suppliers is limited to one. This is generally true of white
goods (engineering products). On the other hand, in a highly
competitive structure, the number of accessable suppliers may
be too many, causing confusion and greater decision effort.
This is very true of dry goods, especially clothing. Similarly, a particular supplier industry may be based on principles
of exclusive distribution or manufacturing, and thus reduce the
number of accessable suppliers. This is generally true of
franchised products and private labels.

A second factor which determines supplier accessability is
the relative marketing effort by different suppliers in the industry. For example, some suppliers are more aggressive in
their selling and marketing practice than others; some are national or even international in their business orientation
whereas others are regional or local; some of them extend more
favorable financial terms than others.

Finally, each supplier is likely to carry a positive or
negative corporate image due to its country of origin, its
business practices and the quality of its products. I believe
that the corporate image is a very significant factor in reducing the list of suppliers regardless of the marketing effort
put forth by the supplier. For example, many perfectly legitimate suppliers from the third world countries are simply ruled
out from consideration due to the negative country image. On
the other hand, suppliers from countries such as Japan and West
Germany carry extra image advantages due to positive image of
their countries. Similarly, the quality of its products may
also generate positive or negative corporate image. For example, names such as Rolls Royce, Nikon, Coca-Cola, IBM, and

184

similar others carry certain image clout in the mind of the retailer.

Supplier accessability, therefore, represents the product/ supplier choices available to the retailer to satisfy his merchandise requirements.

Choice Calculus

It refers to the choice rules or heuristics practiced by different retailers as a way of matching their merchandise requirements and supplier accessability. It reflects the strategic purchasing policy of the retail establishment, so to speak. Based on the more recent knowledge in the area of information processing (Einhorn, 1970; Wright, 1972; Sheth and Raju, 1973; Bettman, 1978), the theory of merchandise buying behavior identifies three distinct choice rules retailers are likely to follow in matching their merchandise requirements and supplier accessability.

The first is a trade-off choice calculus by which the retailer is willing to make trade-offs between various choice criteria such as price, packaging and delivery. Thus, a supplier with better price but worse delivery schedule may be considered as an option along with another supplier with higher price but better delivery schedule. The trade-off calculus, therefore, implies that price and delivery in the above example can be traded or compensated. What matters is the overall average performance of different suppliers on a number of choice criteria.

A second choice rule is called the dominant choice calculus by which the retailer makes choices of suppliers and/or products on one and only one choice criterion. It can be price, delivery, packaging or assortment. However, only those suppliers who meet or exceed the minimum requirements on a dominant criterion such as delivery or price are even considered by the retailer. Then, a supplier who is perceived to be the best on that criterion is selected. Notice that there is no trade-off between the dominant criterion and other criteria.

A third heuristic is called the sequential choice calculus. The retailer has multiple criteria, and based on their relative importance, he sequentially narrows down the supplier options. For example, he may utilize the three criteria of price, delivery and financing in that order of relative importance. Any supplier who does not meet his minimum price is eliminated from considered no matter how good he is on delivery or financing. Among those who meet his price minimums, some are now removed from consideration because they cannot meet his delivery criteria, and selection is made of that supplier who

185

offers the best financing arrangements.

Although there are several other choice rules, it seems that the above three are most prevalent in business practice. Of course, one retailer may prefer one choice calculus and another may prefer a different one. In fact, it is more meaningful to segment the merchandise buyers (retailers) on the type of choice calculus they utilize than on their demographics or consumption behavior. This is because it enables the suppliers to directly target their selling and marketing efforts much more precisely and effectively.

Ideal Supplier/Product Choice

This represents the best choice of a supplier and/or product from among those accessable to the retailer to satisfy his merchandise requirements. It is the outcome of the matching process between merchandise requirements and supplier accessability with the use of any of the three choice calculus. It is labeled as the ideal choice since it represents the outcome of a rational and formal decision-making process. It represents what should be the choice of a supplier and/or product given the merchandise requirements and supplier accessability. Therefore, it can be used as a normative standard with which to compare the actual choice behavior of the retailer. Any discrepancy between the ideal and the actual choice thus represents potential for improvement and greater profitability for the retailer.

Actual Supplier/Product Choice

It represents the actual choice of a supplier or product made by the retailer. In the absence of any other factor which can influence the choice decision, actual supplier/product choice should mirror the ideal supplier/product choice.

However, a number of ad hoc situational factors do intervene in the supplier/product selection process, and motivate the retailer to select another supplier/product which is not the ideal choice. I have grouped these ad hoc situational factors into four categories: business climate, business negotiations, company's financial position and market disturbance.

Business climate refers to the macro economic trends such as recession, inflation, interest rates and unemployment. Despite macro economic theory, it is very difficult to model their impact on supplier/product choices. Sure, we can make some general statements such as in a recessionary period, the retailer is likely to lean toward a supplier who is willing to sell smaller quantities, shorter lead time and more economically; or that high interest rates will motivate the retailer to buy from a supplier who is lenient on credit or who is willing to sell the products on consignment rather than outright sale. However, the volatility and uncertainty is too great to subject the impact of business climate on supplier/product choice to any formal model.

Business negotiations represent the buyer-seller interaction process (Sheth, 1975). They include the tactical aspects of contractual agreements and procurement process. Again, the actual supplier/product choice may deviate from the ideal choice simply because the business negotiations break down or cannot be worked out for whatever reason between the buyer and the seller in the marketplace.

Company's financial position represents the profitability and liquidity position of the retailer. It is a highly dynamic and uncertain situational factor and, therefore, not amenable to either forecasting or model building. However, it does affect the supplier/product choice. For example, when a retailer is highly profitable but does not have liquidity, he is likely to lean toward longer term contracts with better credit terms. On the other hand, if the retailer is not profitable but has a lot of liquidity, he is more likely to lean toward a supplier who is anxious to sell in large quantities at near cost prices.

The last ad hoc situational factor is called the market disturbance. It includes totally unexpected but significant events such as a strike, economic blockade, political turbulence or some natural disaster which all have an impact on the buying decision.

The ad hoc situational factors are separated from other choice determinants because their influence on buying decisions cannot be anticipated or modeled. In that sense, actual supplier/product choice behavior represents the outcome of a contingency (conditional) analysis, whereas the ideal supplier/product choice behavior represents the outcome of a stable (consistent) analysis. I strongly believe that the two processes should not be grouped together partly because their managerial marketing implications are radically different and partly because they require different statistical modeling procedures. In fact, the controversy over stochastic versus deterministic basis for buyer preferences and choice behaviors can be better resolved if we are willing to separate the stable from situational determinants of choices. For example, a significant discrepancy between ideal and actual supplier/product choice is a good indication of situational influences. In that case, a stochastic approach to modeling the merchandise buying behavior is likely to give better results. On the other hand, if the discrepancy between ideal and actual supplier/product choice is minimal or nonexisting, then a deterministic approach to modeling is likely to give better results.

CONCLUSION

There is no question that we need a theory of merchandise buying behavior since none exists today. Furthermore, it would enable us to understand how buying behavior varies across different strata in the marketplace from the producer to the ultimate consumer. It would be pleasantly nice if the same theory can be applied at all the three strata of buying behavior, namely producers, retailers and consumers. If not, the specificity of a stratum should explain the differences.

In any case, the theory of merchandise buying behavior consisting of merchandise requirements, supplier accessability, choice calculus, and ad hoc situations which create discrepancy between actual and ideal choices seems broad enough to attempt a vertical integration in developing a general theory of buying behavior in the marketplace.

REFERENCES

Bettman, James R. (1978), An Information Processing Theory of Consumer Choice, Reading, Mass: Addison-Wesley.

Einhorn, Hillel J. (1970), "The Use of Nonlinear, Noncompensatory Models in Decision-Making," Psychological Bulletin, 75, 221-30.

Engel, James; Roger Blackwell and David Kollat (1978), Consumer Behavior, Third Edition, Hinsdale, Ill: The Dryden Press.

Ferber, Robert, ed. (1977), Selected Aspects of Consumer Behavior, Washington, D.C: U. S. Government Printing Press.

Howard, John A. and Jagdish N. Sheth (1969), The Theory of Buyer Behavior, New York, N. Y.: John Wiley & Sons.

Sheth, Jagdish N. (1975), "Buyer-Seller Interaction: A Conceptual Framework," in Advances in Consumer Behavior, Volume Three, Beverly B. Anderson, ed., Cincinnati, Ohio; Association for Consumer Research, 382-86.

_____ (1977), "Recent Developments in Organizational Buying Behavior," in Consumer and Industrial Buying Behavior, A. G. Woodside, J. N. Sheth and P. D. Bennett, eds., New York N. Y., North-Holland, 17-34.

_____ (1979), "The Surpluses and Shortages in Consumer Behavior Theory and Research," Journal of the Academy of Marketing Science, 4 (Fall), 414-27.

_____, and P. S. Raju (1973), "Sequential and Cyclical Nature of Information Processing Models in Repetitive Choice Behavior," In Advances in Consumer Behavior, Volume One, Scott Ward and Peter Wright, eds., Urbana, Ill.: Association for Consumer Research, 348-58.

Webster, Fred and Yoram Wind (1972), Organizational Buying Behavior, New York, N. Y.: Prentice-Hall.

Wright, Peter (1972), "Consumer Judgment Strategies: Beyond the Compensatory Assumption," in Proceedings of the Third Annual Conference of the Association for Consumer Research, M. Venkatesan, ed., Amherst, Mass." Association for Consumer Research, 316-24.

14/96